The Media-Savvy M Classroom

The Media-Savvy Middle School Classroom is a practical guide for teachers of Grades 5-8 who want to help their students achieve mastery of media literacy skills. Today's fake news, alternative facts, and digital manipulations are compromising the critical thinking and well-being of middle grade learners already going through significant personal changes. This actionable book prepares teachers to help their students become informed consumers of online resources. Spanning correct source use, personal versus expert opinions, deliberate disinformation, social media, and more, these ready-to-use activities can be integrated directly into existing language arts and mathematics lesson plans.

Susan Brooks-Young is an educational consultant at S.J. Brooks-Young Consulting. She has been involved for decades in the field of instructional technology as a teacher, site administrator, and technology specialist.

The Media-Savvy Middle School Classroom

Strategies for Teaching Against Disinformation

Susan Brooks-Young

NEW YORK AND LONDON

First published 2021
by Routledge
52 Vanderbilt Avenue, New York, NY 10017

and by Routledge
2 Park Square, Milton Park, Abingdon, Oxon, OX14 4RN

Routledge is an imprint of the Taylor & Francis Group, an informa business

© 2021 Susan Brooks-Young

The right of Susan Brooks-Young to be identified as author of this work has been asserted by her in accordance with sections 77 and 78 of the Copyright, Designs and Patents Act 1988.

All rights reserved. No part of this book may be reprinted or reproduced or utilised in any form or by any electronic, mechanical, or other means, now known or hereafter invented, including photocopying and recording, or in any information storage or retrieval system, without permission in writing from the publishers.

Trademark notice: Product or corporate names may be trademarks or registered trademarks, and are used only for identification and explanation without intent to infringe.

Library of Congress Cataloging-in-Publication Data
Names: Brooks-Young, Susan, author.
Title: The media-savvy middle school classroom : strategies for teaching against disinformation / Susan Brooks-Young.
Description: Abingdon, Oxon ; New York, NY : Routledge, 2021. | Includes bibliographical references and index.
Identifiers: LCCN 2020016219 (print) | LCCN 2020016220 (ebook) | ISBN 9780367418151 (hardback) | ISBN 9780367420796 (paperback) | ISBN 9780367821616 (ebook)
Subjects: LCSH: Media literacy--Study and teaching (Middle school)
Classification: LCC P96.M4 B76 2021 (print) | LCC P96.M4 (ebook) | DDC 372.34--dc23
LC record available at https://lccn.loc.gov/2020016219
LC ebook record available at https://lccn.loc.gov/2020016220

ISBN: 978-0-367-41815-1 (hbk)
ISBN: 978-0-367-42079-6 (pbk)
ISBN: 978-0-367-82161-6 (ebk)

Typeset in Bembo
by SPi Global, India

Contents

	List of Tables	vi
1	Why These Skills? Why Now?	1
2	Who Said That and Why Does It Matter?	6
3	Who's an Expert?	12
4	Information Echo Chambers	19
5	Fact or Fiction?	26
6	Before You Share	33
7	Can You Believe That?	40
8	Those Pesky Averages	47
9	Framing the Question	54
10	Putting a Slant on Things	60
11	What are the Chances?	67
12	Going Forward	74
	Index	79

Tables

11.1 Survey Results   70

1 Why These Skills? Why Now?

Do you remember when you first heard the term "fake news?" Although many people associate the idea of fake news with the 2016 presidential election in the United States, Jane E. Kirtley, Silha Professor of Media Ethics and Law at the Hubbard School of Journalism and Mass Communication at the University of Minnesota, reminds us that this is not a recent concept. She traces use of the specific term "lying press" back to 1930s Nazi Germany. However, intentional publication of information designed to mislead the public goes back even further in time (Burston et al.). If that's the case, why do people today appear to be more aware of disinformation and less confident about their ability to identify it than they may have been previously?

It's tempting to try to identify a single cause of the current proliferation of disinformation, but the reality is that this is a complex issue. Yes, members of the Trump Administration regularly suggest that "alternate facts" must be given credence and accuse mainstream media of promoting misinformation, but this problem is not confined to the United States. Nor is disinformation confined solely to political issues. Here are just a few examples:

- In 2018, the Muslim co-owner of a restaurant in Ampara, Sri Lanka was badly beaten, his restaurant wrecked, and the local mosque burned because a customer found a lump of flour in his dinner. Unknown to the owner, a fabricated story posted on Facebook the previous day claimed that Muslims were trying to suppress the Buddhist population of Sri Lanka by slipping sterilization drugs into food served in restaurants. The customer mistook the flour for medication (Taub and Fisher).
- A 4-year-old child in Pueblo, Colorado died from influenza because his mother did not give him medication that was prescribed by his physician. Instead she decided to follow the advice of members of an anti-vax Facebook group who recommended natural remedies (Capitides).
- At the height of COVID-19 spread, two companies in the UK were prohibited from publishing online ads for face masks. Britain's Advertising Standards Authority (ASA) determined that the ads violated their code of ethics because they were grounded in fearmongering and misled consumers about the masks' effectiveness in protecting against the virus ("Face mask ads banned").

2 *Why These Skills? Why Now?*

- On a lighter note, in 2014, the company that produces the Red Bull beverage settled a $13 million lawsuit that claimed false advertising was in play when the company used the slogan "Red Bull gives you wings." Clearly, drinking any beverage does not give a person wings, but the person who filed suit claimed the slogan implied that Red Bull was superior to other energy drinks when, in fact, a cup of coffee contains more caffeine than does an 8.4 oz can of Red Bull. The company stated it settled out of court to avoid high court costs.

Here are a few of the factors that make it easier for us to believe disinformation and increase the likelihood that people will believe lies:

- Humans tend to misremember their original sources of information. For instance, a person may have positive thoughts about a product, forgetting that the basis of those feelings comes from having viewed an advertisement, rather than from personal experience (Matthews).
- Headlines are powerful memory triggers. Individuals or organizations that generate disinformation know their consumers are more likely to remember headlines than the text of articles they read. This is the case even when the article demonstrates that the headline is mostly, even completely inaccurate (Jaffe). This is one reason why clickbait is useful for spreading disinformation.
- Repeating inaccurate information is another effective way to get people to believe something that is not true. This is called the "illusory truth effect." It means that our brains respond to information repeated over and over again as though it is true. Both politicians and marketing experts are well aware of this (Dreyfuss).

In addition, we now have access to a wide range of technologies developed within the last decade which facilitates anytime, anywhere delivery of targeted disinformation to specific people. A proliferation of radio and cable television stations that broadcast programming 24/7 also increases the ability to deliver continuous streams of disinformation in many formats. Finally, due to shifting priorities handed down through mandates at the local, state, and federal levels, educators are focusing on basic academics and test scores. They have little or no time left in the school day to teach the skills students need to adequately deal with the amounts of information they encounter daily. And truth be told, many adults also find themselves struggling with differentiating between fact and fiction.

So what is the solution? We can begin acknowledging that despite the reality that technology has become a delivery system for disinformation, the challenges we face in this area will not be solved with technology. This is a problem that requires human intervention. Common sense and critical thinking skills coupled with knowledge of civics and information literacy skills would go a long way toward helping people become better informed consumers of information (Anderson and Rainie).

Why does this book target middle school educators and their students? My experiences as a middle school teacher and site administrator taught me that these students are a unique group. They experience significant shifts in their thinking and world view as they make the transition from elementary to high school. At this age students care deeply about peer relationships, but are also increasingly curious about the world around them. They struggle to make meaning of what they are learning and are willing to push boundaries to do this, but also rely on the adults in their lives to be role models for them.

The findings in Common Sense Media's 2017 report *News and America's Kids*, which examines news consumption among US tweens (ages 10–12) and teens (ages 13–18), underscore the characteristics of middle schoolers described above. For example:

- Nearly one-half of tweens (49%) say that following the news is important to them because it does impact their lives.
- 45% of tweens say that the news frightens them or makes them feel depressed.
- Just 44% of all students surveyed report they are confident they can identify misinformation in the news.
- And, although more survey participants said they prefer getting news from social media sources rather than other sources, they place their greatest trust in news they get from their parents (66%) and teachers (48%).

Given their high interest in following and understanding the news as young as age 10 and the fact that students this age want their learning to be relevant to things they care about, it makes sense to ensure that we are teaching middle school students the skills they need to be good consumers of media. As students' most trusted role models, parents also need to take responsibility for helping their children recognize misinformation. However, many parents look to their child's school for help in this area because they lack the skills necessary to accurately identify misinformation. Educators must step up to help students and parents expand their knowledge and understanding of civics and information literacy.

Does this mean adding one more thing to busy teachers' already packed days? It doesn't have to. Teachers can opt to model responsible citizenship and information literacy skills every day within the context of whatever content skills are being taught. This book helps educators identify key information literacy skills to present in one activity and then incorporate on an ongoing basis. It does this by offering foundational information with an accompanying self-contained activity that can be used as is or modified to meet specific local needs. These concepts may be taught in any order and aligned with existing curricula. Educators may also chose to read a chapter, walk through the activity personally, and then

4 *Why These Skills? Why Now?*

incorporate the focus skills into existing students activities they already plan to use in class.

In addition, covering these strategies is not the responsibility of one teacher—educators can (and should) team up with one another to introduce the activities provided in the book to their students. For example, teachers of language arts and mathematics might work with the library/media specialist to each take responsibility for teaching a few—but not all—of the activities. The ideas in the book can also be used to develop a 10–12-week elective wheel course or a before/after school information literacy program.

One of the important features of this book is its emphasis on the information teachers need to know and understand in order to help their students learn the skills they require to be responsible consumers of media. Educators are provided background information on ten strategies they can use personally and in their classrooms to review information with a discerning eye. Along with opening and closing chapters, ten chapters explore topics related to information literacy and media—five focus on English/Language Arts skills, and five on Mathematics skills. The targeted skills are influenced by the work of Daniel J. Levitin, PhD, who wrote *Weaponized Lies: How to Think Critically in the Post-Truth Era* while teaching a university-level critical thinking course. Chapters 2 through 11 each include a discussion of the targeted skill area for that chapter and a related standards-based activity teachers can use themselves and/or with students, built on consistent sections listed here: Why this is Important; Real Life Examples; Practice; Activity Plan; Questions for Reflection; and, Resources.

There is no "right" way to use the material in this book. The important thing is to review the material yourself and share it with students, their parents, and your colleagues. We each have a responsibility to help ourselves and others learn these critical 21st-century information literacy skills.

Resources

Articles

Anderson, J. and Rainie, L. "The Future of Truth and Misinformation Online." Pew Research Center. October 19, 2017. https://www.pewresearch.org/internet/2017/10/19/the-future-of-truth-and-misinformation-online/. Accessed on March 4, 2020.

Burston, A., et al. "A Citizen's Guide to Fake News." Center for Information Technology & Society, University of California Santa Barbara. August 29, 2018. https://www.cits.ucsb.edu/fake-news. Accessed on March 3, 2020.

Capatides, C. "4-Year-Old Dies from Flu after Members of Anti-Vax Facebook Group Advise His Mom to Use Thyme and Elderberries instead of Tamiflu." *CBS News.* February 7, 2020. https://www.cbsnews.com/news/4-year-old-dies-from-flu-after-members-of-anti-vax-facebook-group-advise-his-mom-use-thyme-elderberries-instead/. Accessed on March 3, 2020.

Dreyfuss, E. "Want To Make a Lie Seem True? Say It Again. And Again. And Again." *Wired.* February 11, 2017. https://www.wired.com/2017/02/dont-believe-lies-just-people-repeat/. Accessed on March 4, 2020.

ITV Report. "Face Mask Ads Banned for 'Scaremongering' and 'Misleading' Coronavirus Claims." *Express and Star News*. March 4, 2020. https://metro.co.uk/2020/03/04/face-mask-ads-banned-misleading-coronavirus-claims-12344412/. Accessed on March 4, 2020.

Jaffe, E. "Misleading Headlines Can Leave Lasting Impressions, Even If You Read the Article." Fast Company. October 28, 2014. https://www.fastcompany.com/3037742/misleading-headlines-can-leave-lasting-impressions-even-if-you-read-the-article. Accessed on March 4, 2020.

Kirtley, J.E. "Getting to the Truth: Fake News, Libel Laws, and 'Enemies of the American People'." American Bar Association. N.D. https://www.americanbar.org/groups/crsj/publications/human_rights_magazine_home/the-ongoing-challenge-to-define-free-speech/getting-to-the-truth/. Accessed on March 3, 2020.

Matthews, J. "A Cognitive Scientist Explains Why Humans Are So Susceptible to Fake News and Misinformation." Nieman Lab. April 17, 2019. https://www.niemanlab.org/2019/04/a-cognitive-scientist-explains-why-humans-are-so-susceptible-to-fake-news-and-misinformation/. Accessed on March 4, 2020.

"News and America's Kids: How Young People Perceive and Are Impacted by the News." Common Sense Media. https://www.commonsensemedia.org/research/news-and-americas-kids. Accessed on March 4, 2020.

Rothman, M. "Red Bull to Pay $13 Million for False Advertising Settlement." BevNET. August 5, 2014. https://www.bevnet.com/news/2014/red-bull-to-pay-13-million-for-false-advertising-settlement/. Accessed on March 4, 2020.

Taub, A. and Fisher, M. "Where Countries Are Tinderboxes and Facebook Is a Match." *The New York Times*. April 21, 2018. https://www.nytimes.com/2018/04/21/world/asia/facebook-sri-lanka-riots.html. Accessed on March 4, 2020.

2 Who Said That and Why Does It Matter?

People frequently quote an expert or authority to lend credibility to a point they are making verbally or in writing. In part, they do this because quotations are easy to remember but also because other people may be more likely to believe something they think was said by a trustworthy individual. The problem is that quotes are regularly misattributed or just downright wrong. This chapter lays the groundwork for educators to strengthen their own skills in vetting quotations they read or hear and provides an activity readers can use as a brush up for themselves and in the classroom to help their students think critically about quotations they read or hear. Questions for reflection and a list of suggested resources completes the chapter.

Why Is This Important?

People are exposed to an astonishing amount of information every day. It's challenging to wade through everything we could be reading, listening to, or viewing, let alone think about what's being said and if it's accurate. This is especially true when we encounter material about unfamiliar topics. How do we know if it's true?

Most of us don't have time to fact-check everything we read or hear. That means we may need to rely on use of other strategies to seek determine the accuracy of the information we come across. Throughout this book, readers are afforded opportunities to explore tactics they can use to vet information they find in the media. In this chapter the focus is on expertise as it is demonstrated by the use of quotations—things said or written by people considered to be authorities in their fields. For a more in-depth discussion of what makes someone an expert, please refer to the "Why Is This Important?" section of Chapter 3.

What are common sources of quotations from experts? In the pre-Internet world, people relied on reference books like Bartlett's *Familiar Quotations*, which has been in print since 1855, or the *Oxford Dictionary of Quotations*. Both of these references are still available in print, but can also be found online. *Familiar Quotations* is accessible at http://www.online-literature.com/quotes/quotations.php and *Oxford Dictionary of Quotations* can be found at www.oxfordreference.com, but they are just two of many online collections of famous quotations, some more reliable than others. In addition to online sources devoted to collections of quotes, social media sites are rife with posts quoting famous individuals for a variety of causes or purposes. The difference between many of these online offerings and more traditional collections is that the latter are curated by professional editors who take time to make sure that both the wording of each quote and its attribution are accurate. This is not always the case with online collections.

An additional concern with quotations found online is that social media sites make it all too easy to repost or share misquotes without first verifying sources. As a result, these inaccurate or misattributed quotes may go viral. What's the harm in sharing misquotes or misattributed quotes?

It goes back to the reality that expert quotes are typically used to convince consumers that something is true (or not, depending on the argument being posed by the author or speaker). In fact, when Vassar research librarian Gretchen Lieb was contacted by Daniel J. Levitin in the course of tracking down the origin of a quote he wanted to use for his book *Weaponized Lies*, she responded that quotations are tricky because they are the "literary equivalent of statistics" (Levitin, 126). When the quote used is misrepresented in any way, the person using the quote to make a point is lying to consumers to get them to believe something that is not true. This can have dire consequences for the person being misquoted or for decision-makers who rely on incorrect information when deciding on a course of action.

Real Life Examples

There are a variety of ways that intentional or inadvertent misuse of quotes leads to misunderstandings in the real world. Here are a few examples.

Six-year-old George Washington has been credited with saying to his father, "I cannot tell a lie," as he confessed to chopping down a prized cherry tree. The reality is that this entire story is a myth and these words were never spoken in the context presented. The cherry tree story was made up by a man named Mason Locke Weems who wrote the apocryphal tale to promote the belief that it was Washington's virtue and honesty that helped him rise to become the first president of the United States ("Cherry Tree Myth").

Similarly, most people believe that P.T. Barnum said, "There's a sucker born every minute," but that's not the case (O'Toole). The earliest mentions of this quote, beginning in 1806, are not attributed to anyone. It wasn't until late in the 19th century that Barnum was named as the source, after a series of other men were credited with having said it. Why does Barnum continue to be associated with this quote? Probably because it *sounds* like something he would say. In addition, attributing this cynical remark to him glamorizes his willingness to exploit others for personal gain.

Just a few days after Osama bin Laden was killed, a quote attributed to Martin Luther King spread rapidly across social media networks (The Root Staff). In response to photos of people in the streets celebrating bin Laden's death, someone posted a quote on Twitter and credited Martin Luther King. The quote was, "I mourn the loss of thousands of precious lives, but I will not rejoice in the death of one, not even an enemy." It's probably obvious that the purpose of the misattributed quote was to chastise people who celebrated the death of bin Laden by invoking the spirit of a well-known pacifist. Despite the fact that Dr. King never said this, the incorrect quote continues to resurface online from time to time.

An article called "The Not-So-Crackpot Autism Theory" published in the *New York Times Magazine* in 2002 misrepresented things said by Dr. Neal Halsey, a researcher at Johns Hopkins University who was interviewed about the safety of childhood vaccines. The combination of an article title intended to raise reader concern and quotes reported out of context made it seem that Dr. Halsey agreed that small amounts of mercury found in vaccines could lead to autism when, in fact, he believes just the opposite. As a result, parents of infants and small children may have made decisions about whether or not to vaccinate their children based on misinformation.

In this final example, something Dr. Halsey said was taken out of context with the express purpose of distorting the meaning of his words. This merits further explanation as it is a classic instance of something called *contextomy*. This is defined as "the practice of misquoting someone by shortening the quotation or by leaving out surrounding words or sentences that would place the quotation in context" ("Definition: Contextomy").

Contextomy is commonly used in advertising to deceive consumers. For example, promotional materials for books, movies and plays, restaurants, as well as other venues or products often include quotations that are misleading. Consumers may see a movie trailer that includes a statement from a well-known reviewer along the lines of "Best movie of the season!" when, in fact, what the reviewer said was "If you just don't care about the quality of entertainment any more, you might consider this to be the best movie of the season." Or perhaps it's an ad for a new clothing line that quotes a famous fashion critic saying, "Innovative … appealing … edgy," when the critic actually wrote, "If you're looking for something innovative, appealing, or edgy, you've come to the wrong clothing line!"

These examples are fairly benign. A consumer may regret spending $12 on a movie ticket or $35 for a new shirt that is not well-made, but these are not weighty decisions in the overall scheme of things. That changes when contextomy is used to make a political statement or argue against scientific fact as in the example of the reporting of Dr. Halsey's interview.

Classroom Practice

As a young educator, I taught English/Language Arts classes at the middle school level. I spent time ensuring that students learned strategies they could use to make the material they read more accessible, but I see now that I did not spend enough time on how to read that material critically. Without really thinking about it, I assumed that textbooks (for example) were reviewed and edited carefully so that students didn't need to question the content presented. Sure, mathematics textbooks sometimes included incorrect answers to problems, and any textbook might have a typographical error but I do not remember wondering if the content in general was factually accurate. That was a long time ago and I realize now that I was naïve. Students need to be taught from an early age to read critically and not accept material assigned in class at face value. Even if they don't encounter misinformation in the classroom they need to develop a mindset that recognizes the value of questioning what they read.

Of course, it's not possible or desirable to check every word, but there are things that can be readily vetted like titles, captions, charts, graphs, and quotations. Different chapters of this book include tools educators and students can use to check some of these other features, but the resources listed below specifically target verifying quotations.

1. Quote Investigator (https://quoteinvestigator.com/): This website consists of a searchable database of well-documented short articles that explore the origins of famous quotations.
2. Can't Confirm That Quotation? Search Google Books (https://www.kqed. org/mindshift/19668/cant-confirm-that-quotation-search-google-books): Professional librarian Tasha Bergson-Michelson explains a step-by-step process for tracking down the origins of famous quotations.
3. How to Research a Quotation (https://www.nypl.org/blog/2013/11/22/ how-to-research-quotations): Sharon Rickson (New York Public Library) explains how to track down the source of a quotation and provides a list of online tools that can be used for this purpose.

Begin with the activity described in the Activity Plan section of this chapter, then follow up by challenging students to research quotations they encounter in future reading using the resources and strategies listed above and in the activity below. When they encounter misquotes or misattributions, ask students to take a little time to think about what the author or speaker might have been trying to accomplish by using the quotation in question. Encourage students to check quotations even when they think they know where they came from. Sometimes it's what we think we know that trips us up more readily than what we realize we don't know.

Activity Plan—Verify Quotations

People frequently use quotes to add credibility to a point being made, particularly if they can attribute the quote to someone who is well-known. In part, this because quotes are easy to remember and people tend to believe something when they think it was said by a trustworthy individual. In truth, quotes are regularly misattributed or just downright wrong.

What follows is a description of an activity readers may use themselves or with their students. The full activity plan, including a student handout, is available online in the Instructional Activities section at: http://medialiteracytoday.net.

10 *Who Said That and Why Does It Matter?*

Please feel free to download the activity plan and handout files for ongoing use. This activity can be completed in one or two class sessions depending on the length of the instructional period and students' research skills.

Objective: Given eight quotations, students will identify which are correctly attributed and which are not using on- and offline reference tools.

Standards: CCSS.ELA-LITERACY.RI.6.7-6.9, CCSS.ELA-LITERACY. SL.6.1-6.4, CCSS.ELA-LITERACY.W.6.7, CCSS.ELA-LITERACY.RI.7.8-7.9, CCSS.ELA-LITERACY.SL.7.1-7.4,CCSS.ELA-LITERACY.W.7.7,CCSS.ELA-LITERACY.RI.8.7-8.9, CCSS.ELA-LITERACY.SL.8.1-8.4, CCSS.ELA-LITERACY.W.8.7, CCSS.ELA-LITERACY.WHST.6-8.7

Outline—Set the Stage: To help students understand that people are often fooled by what they *think* they know or by a statement erroneously attributed to an expert, open the activity by discussing the origin of a familiar quote that is actually a misattribution. Here's an example. Who said, "Elementary, my dear Watson?" (It was not Sherlock Holmes, O'Toole.) Explain that savvy media consumers do not accept the authenticity of quotations at face value, particularly when they are used to lend authenticity to an argument or position. This means that media consumers must check to ensure that the quotes they come across are accurately worded and attributed.

Outline—Activity: In small groups or as a whole class, brainstorm ideas for strategies to use to verify the origins and accuracy of quotations. Select four or five of the strategies listed and use them to determine the authenticity of one famous quote (choose your own or use a quote provided on the student handout at https://www.medialiteracytoday.net/). Students who are successful at verifying the accuracy/origin of the first quote continue working in their small groups. Teacher may provide addition support to students who need to be led through another example. When the activity is complete, student teams will have correctly vetted the authenticity of eight quotations. An answer key is provided in the activity plan.

Outline—Extension: Provide copies of on- or offline newspaper articles that include one or more quotations. Ask students to check their authenticity and share their findings with the class.

To help students make a habit of not taking quotations at face value, encourage them to continue checking the origins of quotations they encounter in their reading. Hold a weekly challenge where students bring in one quotation they checked in the previous seven days along with their determination if it was accurately attributed or not.

Questions for Reflection

1. What are the most important ideas presented in this chapter, both for educators and for students?
2. How will you model the skills described in this chapter to ensure your students understand the importance of checking the accuracy and origins of quotations?

3. How will you continue to hold students accountable for vetting the accuracy and origins of quotations?
4. How will the information presented in this chapter impact how you interact with quotations you read and share in social media?

Resources

Articles

"Definition: Contextomy." Dictionary.com. https://www.dictionary.com/browse/contextomy. Accessed on September 21, 2019.

"Neal Halsey Reaffirms Vaccines Do Not Cause Autism." Johns Hopkins Bloomberg School of Public Health. November 14, 2002. https://www.jhsph.edu/news/news-releases/2002/halsey-autism.html. Accessed on July 22, 2020.

O'Toole, G. "There's a Sucker Born Every Minute." Quote Investigator. April 11, 2014. https://quoteinvestigator.com/2014/04/11/fool-born/. Accessed on September 26, 2019.

Richardson, J. "Cherry Tree Myth." George Washington's Mount Vernon. https://www.mountvernon.org/library/digitalhistory/digital-encyclopedia/article/cherry-tree-myth/. Accessed on September 26, 2019.

The Root Staff. "Fake MLK Quote Goes Viral." *The Root*. May 3, 2011. https://www.theroot.com/fake-mlk-quote-goes-viral-1790863806. Accessed on September 21, 2019.

Books

Levitin, D.J. *Weaponized Lies: How to Think Critically in the Post-Truth Era*. New York: Dutton, 2017.

Chapter 2 Activity

Bergson-Michelson, T. "Can't Confirm That Quotation? Search Google Books." MindShift. March 7, 2012. https://www.kqed.org/mindshift/19668/cant-confirm-that-quotation-search-google-books. Accessed on September 21, 2019.

"List of Famous Misquotations." Wikiquote. N.D. https://en.wikiquote.org/wiki/List_of_famous_misquotations. Accessed on September 21, 2019.

O'Toole, G. "Elementary, My Dear Watson." *Quote Investigator*. 2016. https://quoteinvestigator.com/2016/07/14/watson/. Accessed on October 1, 2019.

O'Toole, G. "What We Have Once Enjoyed We Can Never Lose ... All That We Love Deeply Becomes a Part of Us." Quote Investigator. 2019. https://quoteinvestigator.com. Accessed on September 21, 2019.

Rickson, S. "How to Research a Quotation." New York Public Library. November 22, 2013. https://www.nypl.org/blog/2013/11/22/how-to-research-quotations. Accessed on September 21, 2019.

Sullivan, J. "Misquotes: Searching for Authenticity Online." Finding Dulcinea. October 27, 2011. http://www.findingdulcinea.com/features/edu/Misquotes--Searching-for-Authenticity-Online.html. Accessed on September 21, 2019.

3 Who's an Expert?

People often cite experts to add credibility to an idea they support. A bonafide expert is someone who knows a lot about one or more specific topics. When bonafide experts are asked for an opinion about something related to their fields of study, they will analyze the facts and most likely offer accurate information. But experts do sometimes make mistakes, especially when they offer opinions about topics outside their fields of study. This chapter lays the groundwork for educators to strengthen their own skills in deciding if someone is an expert in a field and if that person is making a statement based on an analysis of facts or personal opinion. It also provides an activity readers can use to review their own skills at evaluating expert opinions and in the classroom to help students think critically about expert opinions they read or hear. Questions for reflection and a list of suggested resources completes the chapter.

Why Is This Important?

Expert is defined in several ways. According to Dictionary.com, an expert is "a person who has special skill or knowledge in some particular field; specialist; authority: *a language expert*." Business dictionary defines expert as a "Professional who has acquired knowledge and skills through study and practice over the years, in a particular field or subject, to the extent that his or her opinion may be helpful in fact finding, problem solving, or understanding of a situation." And Fernand Gobet writes that an expert is "somebody who obtains results that are vastly superior to those obtained by the majority of the population" (Gobet and Ereku).

How does one become an expert? According to Ericsson et al., experts are not born—they are made through dedicated study and practice. Furthermore, the criteria for becoming an expert changes from one field to the next as do the skills or knowledge required to achieve superior results. For example, becoming an expert in a field like general surgery requires a combination of academic knowledge and years of practice in actually performing various surgeries, while an expert in American history may gain their knowledge through academic study at the post-graduate level coupled with travel. Successful sports figures or entertainers become experts in their fields through years of practice, but also benefit from studying strategies or techniques they can use to improve their performance.

However, completing an academic course of study or practicing skills over and over does not necessarily make a person an expert. We've all heard stories about athletes who wanted to become professional football players or dancers but didn't have the physical strength or agility to excel in their chosen sport. We know that a diploma or certificate in a specific field may—or may not—indicate expertise on the part of the recipient. This is because just a handful of the people who complete undergraduate or advanced degree programs do so at the top of their class—the vast majority of graduates are competent, but average.

Ericsson et al. write that there are three tests of real expertise. The first test supports the statement in Gobet and Ereku's definition of experts that these are people who achieve vastly superior results when compared to most people. The second test of expertise is whether or not concrete results are achieved. In other words, a person can have great theories, but to be a true expert that individual must also be able to demonstrate positive outcomes of his/her work. For example, an educator may claim to be an expert in the implementation of a new instructional strategy, but must also be able to document successful use of the strategy with students based on commonly accepted measures of student achievement. The final test of real expertise is whether or not an expert's results can be replicated. This is easily done in settings where skill or knowledge is demonstrated through some type of competition, but it is also possible to assess less easily measured skillsets through use of scenarios or rubrics that rate someone's level of proficiency at completing a task.

Two additional truths muddy the waters even further. First, not all experts in the same field always agree with one another leaving us to decide who we can believe and why. And second, even those who achieve expertise in one field are not necessarily experts in other areas. There's actually a term for a person who "criticizes, judges, or gives advice outside the area of his or her expertise." He or she is known as an ultracrepidarian ("Definition: ultracrepidarian"). In today's world with the vast amount of information published every day, it is increasingly difficult to separate experts from ultracrepidarians.

Real Life Examples

If you've ever listened to a panel of "experts" dissect a breaking news story, rehash last weekend's football game, or review the latest blockbuster film, you've had first-hand experience of real life examples of why it's important to understand the ways these opinions are used to influence viewers' feelings about the event, game, or movie. The people who sit on these panels are called *pundits*. Just as there are several definitions for the term expert, pundit is defined in more than one way. Multiple dictionaries actually offer two meanings for pundit as in the case of this Cambridge Dictionary definition which reads "a person who knows a lot about a particular subject, or someone who gives opinions in a way that sounds intelligent or wise." In other words, an expert may also be a pundit, but a pundit isn't always an actual expert.

14   *Who's an Expert?*

This is an important distinction in today's media environment where a 24-hour news cycle is often fleshed out through use of pundits. How did this become the case? Let's take a quick look at news and the media.

Prior to the invention of the printing press, people generally got news through word of mouth or letters in the case of people who were literate or who had access to scribes. Once the printing press was available, print material of all kinds became more common. This included publications that offered news, but newspapers as we think of them became common during the 19th century.

The first known newscast was broadcast on WWJ, a radio station launched by the E.W. Scripps Company, publisher of *The Detroit News* on August 31, 1920. At that time, people were trying to sort out exactly what radio's role would be in entertaining and/or informing listeners. On the off-chance that radio might make print newspapers obsolete, the company decided to give an all-news radio format a try. Although it didn't put the newspaper out of business, WWJ was a success and still operates today using the same all-news format (Abell). In 1940, the first televised newscast was hosted on an NBC station based in New York City, WNBT. It was a simulcast of Lowell Thomas' radio newscast.

Over the ensuing 40 years or so, televised newscasts expanded from 15 to 30 minutes and then to 60 minutes. Other types of news-based programs also cropped up, but conventional wisdom tells us it was cable-news networks that launched the 24-hour news cycle. First CNN and then FOX and MSNBC—we are now able to access news-based programming around the clock (Hansen). The problem with this is that there simply isn't that much news to report, so networks keep viewers tuned in by offering interviews, panel discussions, news magazines, and other programming designed specifically to keep viewership up but also blurring the line between true journalism and entertainment. And there's the rub.

As consumers of cable news, many Americans are not as adept at differentiating between an expert weighing in on a news story and a pundit, who may—or may not—be an expert in the field being discussed. In 2018, the Pew Research Center reported findings from a survey where 44% of respondents said they prefer to watch the news on television, 34% want to get their news online, 14% prefer listening to news on the radio, and just 7% want to read a newspaper (Mitchell). If we are going to get the bulk of our news from television, we need to become better at questioning what we are hearing instead of assuming that all talking heads are equally well-informed and qualified to share their opinions.

Classroom Practice

The discussion in the previous section of this chapter focuses on how experts and pundits are used in the media to influence consumers' thinking about various issues. There are other common situations where expert opinion is very important. For example:

- When researching medical care options patients often seek multiple opinions about which treatment would be best for them.

- Attorneys often bring in experts to give their opinion about critical facts in a case that is being tried in court.
- Prior to making a major purchase like a car, consumers may rely on expert product reviews from respected sources such as Consumer Reports.

While the focus of this book is on how expert opinion is used in the media, it is useful for teachers to take any opportunity to challenge students to recognize when they are being asked to rely on expert opinion about a topic and to ask them to think carefully about how they can decide if the opinion presented is likely to be correct. Different chapters of this book include tools educators and students can use to check some of these other features, but the resources listed below offer tips and/or resources for verifying expert or pundit opinion.

1. When to rely on experts for important decisions (https://www.decision-making-solutions.com/rely-on-experts.html): This article includes a list of nine criteria to use when making decisions. The list is most appropriate for educators who will need to reword it for student use.
2. How do I know if an author is an expert? (https://apus.libanswers.com/faq/131345): Librarian Priscilla Coulter offers advice on how to decide if an article has been written by an expert. Although written for college students, middle schoolers are able to follow these suggestions as well.
3. Understanding and Evaluating Sources (https://nmsu.libguides.com/sources/factcheck): Students can fact-check statements made by experts and pundits. This list of five fact-checking resources is provided by New Mexico University.

Begin with the activity described in the Activity Plan section of this chapter, then follow up by challenging students to think critically about the differences between experts and pundits as well as how these differences might impact their own thinking about various topics. Encourage them to use the resources and strategies listed above and in the activity below. When they encounter experts and pundits sharing their opinions, ask students to take a little time to think about what those people might be trying to accomplish by expressing an opinion. Encourage students to vet experts' backgrounds even when they think they know about the person. It may be that while the person does have expertise in a given field, that they do not have in-depth knowledge about something they are stating an opinion about.

Activity Plan

Activity: People often cite experts to add credibility to an idea they support. A bonafide expert is someone who knows a lot about one or more specific topics. When bonafide experts are asked for an opinion about something related to their fields of study, they will analyze the facts and most likely offer accurate information. But experts do sometimes make mistakes, especially when they

16 *Who's an Expert?*

offer opinions about topics outside their fields of study. How can we decide if someone is an expert in a field and if that person is making a statement based on an analysis of facts or personal opinion?

What follows is a description of an activity readers may use themselves or with their students. The full activity plan including a student handout is available online in the Instructional Activities section at: http://medialiteracytoday.net. Please feel free to download the activity plan and handout files for ongoing use. This activity can be completed in one or two class sessions depending on the length of the instructional period and students' research skills.

Objective: Given several scenarios, students will use on- and offline tools to determine if the opinions shared in those scenarios are, in fact, offered by people considered to be experts in their respective fields and reliable.

Standards: CCSS.ELA-LITERACY.RI.6.7-6.9, CCSS.ELA-LITERACY. SL.6.1-6.4, CCSS.ELA-LITERACY.W.6.7, CCSS.ELA-LITERACY.RI.7.8-7.9, CCSS.ELA-LITERACY.SL.7.1-7.4, CCSS.ELA-LITERACY.W.7.7, CCSS.ELA-LITERACY.RI.8.7-8.9, CCSS.ELA-LITERACY.SL.8.1-8.4, CCSS.ELA-LITERACY.W.8.7, CCSS.ELA-LITERACY.WHST.6-8.7

Outline—Set the Stage: To help students focus on the topic of this learning activity, open the lesson by giving students 4–5 minutes to think individually about what makes a person an expert and write down a few ideas. Next, ask students turn to someone sitting by them to discuss the ideas they wrote down (5–6 minutes). Then, give students a few minutes to revise what they wrote originally. Finally, lead a class discussion in which students share their thinking about what makes someone an expert.

Tell students that the Oxford Dictionary defines an expert as: "A person who is very knowledgeable about or skillful in a particular area. For example, 'an expert in health care' or 'a financial expert'." Compare this definition to points made during the class discussion.

Outline—Activity: Tell students they will work in pairs or trios to review several scenarios taken from real life in which a person who has expertise in one or more fields offers an expert opinion that may, or may not be accurate (create your own scenarios or use those provided on the student handout at: http://medialiteracytoday.net). Students will use three steps as they complete this assignment:

1. **Consider the source:** A link is provided for each scenario. Does the link lead to a reliable source? What can students do to determine reliability?
2. **Check the facts:** Search online or review print reference materials to verify that the event described in the scenario happened as described. Try to find three reliable sources that confirm or deny the facts as presented.
3. **Learn about the expert:** Search online or review print reference materials to learn more about the expert, including his/her areas of expertise and overall career.

Walk the entire class through the first scenario. Students who are successful at determining if the expert opinion is accurate may continue working in their small groups. Teachers may provide additional support to students who need to be led through another example. When the activity is complete, student teams will have correctly determined if the expert opinions shared in various scenarios are, in fact, offered by experts in the related field and reliable. An answer key is provided in the activity plan.

Outline—Extension: There are many topics students can explore to determine if opinions being offered are, in fact, expert opinions that are likely to be accurate. Ask students to brainstorm a list of current issues many people have opinions about that they might want to explore further. For example, they might suggest:

1. What was the underlying cause of the 2019 measles outbreak in WA?
2. Is climate change responsible for increasingly severe storms?
3. What has caused the recent crashes of two Boeing 737 Max 8 planes?
4. Does switching back and forth between Standard Time and Daylight Savings Time really harm people?

Questions for Reflection

1. What are the most important ideas presented in this chapter, both for educators and for students?
2. How will you model the skills described in this chapter to ensure your students understand the importance of determining if a person is actually considered to be an expert in their respective field and reliable?
3. How will you continue to hold students accountable for checking a person's level of expertise and the reliability of opinions being expressed by this person?
4. How will the information presented in this chapter impact how you view statements made by pundits online and on television?

Resources

Articles

Abell, J.C. "Aug. 31, 1920: News Radio Makes News." *Wired.* August 31, 2010. https://www.wired.com/2010/08/0831first-radio-news-broadcast/. Accessed on October 9, 2019.

Coulter, P. "How Can You Tell Which Articles or Books Are Written by an Authority in the Field?" Richard G. Trefry Library. August 31, 2017. https://apus.libanswers.com/faq/131345#:~:text=How%20can%20you%20tell%20which,D.%2C%20Ed. Accessed on October 16, 2019.

"Definition: Expert." Business Dictionary, 2019. http://www.businessdictionary.com/definition/expert.html. Accessed on October 10, 2019.

18 *Who's an Expert?*

"Definition: Expert." Dictionary.com, 2019a. https://www.dictionary.com/browse/expert. Accessed on October 10, 2019a.

"Definition: Pundit." Cambridge Dictionary, 2019. https://dictionary.cambridge.org/us/dictionary/english/pundit. Accessed on October 15, 2019.

"Definition: Ultracrepidarian." Dictionary.com, 2019b. https://www.dictionary.com/browse/ultracrepidarian. Accessed on October 10, 2019b.

Ericsson, K.A., Prietula, M.J., and Cokely, E.T.. "The Making of an Expert." *Harvard Business Review.* July–August 2007. https://hbr.org/2007/07/the-making-of-an-expert. Accessed on October 10, 2019.

Gobet, F. and Ereku, M.H. "What Is Expertise?" *Psychology Today.* February 23, 2016. https://www.psychologytoday.com/us/blog/inside-expertise/201602/what-is-expertise. Accessed on October 9, 2019.

Hansen, L. "The Power of the 24-Hour News Cycle" Weekend Edition Sunday—NPR. May 29, 2005. https://www.npr.org/templates/story/story.php?storyId=4671485. Accessed on October 15, 2019.

Mitchell, A. "Americans Still Prefer Watching to Reading the News—and Mostly Still through Television." Pew Research Center. December 3, 2018. https://www.journalism.org/2018/12/03/americans-still-prefer-watching-to-reading-the-news-and-mostly-still-through-television/. Accessed on October 12, 2019.

"Understanding & Evaluating Sources." New Mexico State University Library. August 13, 2019. https://nmsu.libguides.com/sources/factcheck. Accessed on October 16, 2019.

"When to Rely on Experts for Important Decisions." Decision Innovation, 2019. https://www.decision-making-solutions.com/rely-on-experts.html. Accessed on October 16, 2019.

Chapter 3 Activity

"The Beatles Audition for Decca Records." The Beatles Bible, 2019. https://www.beatlesbible.com/1962/01/01/recording-decca-audition/. Accessed on October 17, 2019.

"Fred Thompson American Advisors Group (AAG) Commercial for Reverse Mortgage." YouTube, 2019. https://www.youtube.com/watch?v=-5Bw3gB7o9E. Accessed on October 17, 2019.

Schrock, K. "The 5Ws of Website Evaluation." Schrock Guide, 2019. http://www.schrockguide.net/uploads/3/9/2/2/392267/schrock_5ws.pdf. Accessed on October 17, 2019.

Shetterly, M.L. "Katherine Johnson Biography." National Aeronautics and Space Administration, 2019. https://www.nasa.gov/content/katherine-johnson-biography. Accessed on October 17, 2019.

Van Helden, A. "Galileo." *Encyclopedia Britannica,* 2019. https://www.britannica.com/biography/Galileo-Galilei. Accessed on October 17, 2019.

4   Information Echo Chambers

Where do most Americans get their news and how many different sources do people use within these platforms? The answer to this question is significant because people tend to gravitate to a few sources that typically echo opinions they already hold. As a result, people end up in an information echo chamber where what they see is heavily slanted toward what they already agree with. This chapter lays the groundwork for educators to examine their personal information echo chambers and includes an activity suitable for readers and students which can be used to help them create a plan to bring more balance to this aspect of their lives. Questions for reflection and a list of suggested resources complete the chapter.

Why Is This Important?

There are two definitions for the term *echo chamber*. The first is "a room or space in which sound echoes." And the second is "a situation in which people only hear opinions of one type, or opinions that are similar to their own" ("Definition: Echo Chamber"). Information echo chambers are also sometimes called personal information bubbles. When learning media literacy skills for today's world, it is critical that we be aware of how people tend to deal with information presented in the media. First, most people gravitate toward information they already agree with. This is called *confirmation bias* ("Definition: Confirmation Bias"). Teachers often see confirmation bias in action when students are doing research for a project or paper. Rather than being open to multiple points of view about the topic being studied, pupils frequently focus on information that confirms what they already think, ignoring different points of view.

There is another relevant bias. We assume that the people around us think the same way we do—this is called *false consensus effect* (Cherry). For example, a few years ago I was having a conversation with another educator I'd recently met. We were discussing safety net social services for students and families. Since we both worked in high-poverty schools, I assumed she held the same beliefs I did about making such services available to families. I was taken aback when I realized that she viewed this practice as encouraging poor decision-making on the part of families, completely disagreeing with my take that it helps level the playing field for people in difficult circumstances. Based on nothing more than the fact that we were both educators, I projected my views on this person.

Everyone experiences these biases to some degree. It's important to mention this here because this is what makes it easy for us to slip into personal information bubbles, limiting our understanding of important issues and what people think about them. This does not mean that there are two sides to every story, because sometimes that simply isn't the case. But it does mean that it's important to keep in mind that all of us are subject to confirmation bias and false consensus effect and take steps to avoid slipping into this kind of thinking. How can we do this?

In his article, "Confirmation Bias: 6 Ways to Recognise It and 5 Ways to Counter It," Ben Allen suggests that just the fact that someone recognizes when they are engaging in this type of behavior can be enough to trigger a change in what that person does next. But what steps can be taken to intentionally reduce the impact of confirmation bias once it's identified? Here are a few suggestions.

1. Research multiple points of view: While researching the topic, read articles from a wide range of reliable resources that present different opinions.
2. Engage in conversations about the topic: Seek out people who hold different opinions on the subject. Ask them to share their ideas with you and listen carefully. Get someone to play devil's advocate if you can't find anyone willing to talk with you about the issue.
3. Walk in the other person's shoes: Consider the topic from another point of view. If you know someone who holds a different opinion, imagine you are that person and that you are researching the same subject. What would you do differently? What resources would you review? What points would you make?
4. Ask yourself, "What if?": If you are engaging in this exercise to make a decision, consider what your choices are and then research your second or third choice to broaden your thinking about the topic.

The point of these activities is not to throw you into analysis paralysis. Instead, the point is to encourage you to get out of your own best thinking and consider other possibilities to help avoid confirmation bias.

What about false consensus effect? How can you avoid slipping into that thinking? Here are some ideas.

1. Avoid making assumptions: Keep in mind that not everyone agrees with you. Be open to understanding how others might think or behave.
2. Examine your own point of view: What are the positive and negative aspects of your viewpoint? Imagine the potential benefits of another point of view.
3. Assess your commitment to your own opinion: Those times when it's especially difficult to consider someone else's opinion, take a moment to gauge

how invested you are in your own thinking being correct. The more you value your own opinion, the harder it will be to consider opposing points of view. Being aware of this may help broaden your own thinking.

While family and friends may hold points of view similar to your own, that's not the case with the wider world. Avoid assuming that your thoughts, beliefs, and/ or values are held by the world at large. Refusing to put yourself into a personal information bubble is one way to do this.

Real Life Examples

Why do we allow ourselves to create and reside in personal information bubbles? In today's world it's easy to allow convenience and a lack of understanding about the algorithms behind digital tools many of us use to access information of all kinds. This is the case whether we're trying to stay up with current events or find other information we'd like to use to make decisions ranging from household purchases to entertainment options.

For example, at a very basic level, many people find it more convenient to shop online than go to a store. At some point users are urged to set up accounts to see sale prices or make actual purchases. Once an account is established, users will notice that every time they return to the site, they see suggestions for what they might want to look at or purchase next, based on what they reviewed or bought previously. When users review earlier purchases, these suggestions may be even better targeted. Yes, it may be more convenient to go with recommendations, but how many other products do users never see because they take the easiest course of action? To learn more about how algorithms are used to target online shoppers, read Graham Charlton's article, "How Online Retailers Can Use Algorithms to Grow Their Business," cited below.

The use of algorithms to target online users becomes even more consequential when we rely on the Internet as a source of news. According to a 2018 survey from Pew Research Center, 34% of American prefer to get their news from online sources. There are apps and online curation tools that allow users to create personal information bubbles by limiting sources and topics of the articles they read. Social media platforms also use algorithms to determine what political and other news users see based on who their friends on that platform are and their own behavior on the site—what they've liked or hidden, for example (Mitchell et al.) If people don't understand how this works, it's entirely possible for them to reside in an online echo chamber without realizing what's happening.

People also create information echo chambers offline. They get their news from the same television stations or radio stations every day. They consistently read the same newspapers or periodicals. A steady diet of anything limits anyone's world view. It's critical that we watch, listen to, or read things that present

22 *Information Echo Chambers*

points of view not already our own. Not necessarily because we need to change our minds, but because we do need to understand where other people are coming from, how they are thinking, and why.

Classroom Practice

Helping students avoid information echo chambers is an ongoing process that involves direct instruction and modeling. Here are two suggestions. First, students increasingly use Internet browsers and search engines for online research, but often do not understand how these tools work. Prior to assigning a research project, review the following tips with students.

- Browsers track users' search histories. Clearing cookies and the browser cache enables users to see results that do not reflect their search history.
- Using different browsers allows users to see different search results.
- Use different search tools within the browser. For example, Google, Bing, and DuckDuckGo are three search engines that work within a browser.
- The type of device used can alter a search. For example, a search conducted on a smartphone may yield different results from a search done on a laptop.
- Location will impact the results. For example, users in the USA are less likely to see links to websites based in other countries.

Additional information about how Internet searches work is available here:

1. How Internet Search Engines Work (https://computer.howstuffworks. com/internet/basics/search-engine.htm): HowStuffWorks offers clear explanations of complex ideas.
2. The Internet: How Search Works (https://www.youtube.com/watch?v=L VV_93mBfSU&feature=youtu.be): This video provides an explanation of how search engines work that is accessible to middle schoolers.
3. Sources and Search Engines (https://curriculum.code.org/csd-1718/ unit2/12/):This lesson plan can be used with the video listed above to help students think about online search strategies.

Second, a critical strategy for breaking out of an information echo chamber is the ability to think about something from another person's point of view. This skill is grounded in one's capacity to empathize with others. Educators increasingly recognize that students who are able to empathize with others reap many benefits, both academic and personal. In the context of this chapter, give students opportunities to practice empathy by creating activities where they are asked to consider someone else's point of view. For example, ask students to retell a story from a secondary character's point or view or ask students to bring current event articles that describe the same incident from different points of view. It takes a little time and practice, but your efforts will pay off tenfold.

Activity Plan

Activity: Information Echo Chambers—Where do most Americans get their news? Identifying the news platforms people use—e.g., TV or print—is helpful, but it's not the only important thing to know. Another critical question is how many different sources do people use within these platforms? This is significant because people tend to gravitate to a few sources that typically echo opinions they already hold. People watch just one news channel, listen to just one radio station, or read just one newspaper because the information provided conforms to their existing biases. Social media exaggerates this situation because the algorithms that drive new posts to individuals' feeds are designed to keep those users on sites as long as possible. This is accomplished by showing users new content that has been selected just for them. As a result, people end up in an information echo chamber where what they see is heavily slanted toward what they already agree with. It's up to consumers to break out of these echo chambers to learn about other points of view.

What follows is a description of an activity readers may use themselves or with their students. The full activity plan including a student handout is available online in the Instructional Activities section at: http://medialiteracytoday.net. Please feel free to download the activity plan and handout files for ongoing use. This activity can be completed in one or two class sessions depending on the length of the instructional period and students' research skills.

Objective: Students work in pairs or trios to examine their personal information echo chambers and create a plan to bring more balance to this aspect of their lives.

Standards: CCSS.ELA-LITERACY.RI.6.7-6.9, CCSS.ELA-LITERACY. SL.6.1-6.4, CCSS.ELA-LITERACY.W.6.7, CCSS.ELA-LITERACY.RI.7.8-7.9, CCSS.ELA-LITERACY.SL.7.1-7.4, CCSS.ELA-LITERACY.W.7.7, CCSS. ELA-LITERACY.RI.8.7-8.9, CCSS.ELA-LITERACY.SL.8.1-8.4, CCSS.ELA-LITERACY.W.8.7, CCSS.ELA-LITERACY.WHST.6-8.7

Outline—Set the Stage: Begin the activity with a class discussion about the term "echo chamber" as it relates to news and information in general. Then allow students to work in their pairs or trios to write a definition for this term. Review students' ideas in a whole-class discussion. Explain that responsible media consumers recognize that information echo chambers are built by carefully selecting information geared to the reader's pre-existing beliefs and that it's up to individuals to break out of these echo chambers to read and evaluate differing points of view.

Outline—Activity: This activity is broken into several parts. Students rotate through working individually, in pairs or trios, as a whole class, and then wrap up doing some additional individual work.

Open with a group discussion about where students currently get their news, then give students time to think about ways they access news and to respond individually to the 12 survey questions on the Information Echo Chambers handout. Point out the five questions to be answered independently immediately following the survey and give them time to write a response.

24 *Information Echo Chambers*

Students move into their pairs or trios to share their responses with one another and discuss the four questions posed in the **With your partner(s)** section of the handout. Lead a class discussion about how students currently access news and how they might improve that practice.

Following the class discussion, ask students to write a personal plan for how they will become a better consumer of news. Remind them that the plan must include the following:

1. A statement about how often they plan to access news each week.
2. A list of specific, balanced, and reliable news resources they will use along with an explanation about why they chose these resources.
3. An explanation of how they will hold themselves accountable for following this plan.

Outline—Extension: There are many follow-up activities for students. Here are two suggestions. What was the underlying cause of the 2019 measles outbreak in Washington State?

1. Ask students to learn more about false equivalence by finding examples in the news and sharing these examples in class.
2. Ask students to create a checklist for determining the reliability of news sources.

Questions for Reflection

1. What are the most important ideas presented in this chapter, both for educators and for students?
2. How will you model the skills described in this chapter to ensure your students implement their plans to expand the sources of news they read, listen to, or watch?
3. How can you incorporate use of their plans into all research projects you assign?
4. How will the information presented in this chapter impact your personal efforts to consider multiple points of view when consuming news?

Resources

Articles

Allen, B. "Confirmation Bias: 6 Ways to Recognise It and 5 Ways to Counter It." Techindc. March 20, 2018. https://techindc.com/confirmation-bias/3063/. Accessed on October 22, 2019.

Charlton, G. "How Online Retailers Can Use Algorithms to Grow Their Business." The UK Domain. June 27, 2018. https://www.theukdomain.uk/online-retailers-can-use-algorithms-grow-business/. Accessed on October 28, 2019.

Cherry, K. "How False Consensus Effect Influences the Way We Think about Others." *Verywell Mind.* September 19, 2019. https://www.verywellmind.com/what-is-the-false-consensus-effect-2795030. Accessed on October 23, 2019.

"Definition: Confirmation Bias." Dictionary.com. https://www.dictionary.com/browse/confirmation-bias. Accessed on October 22, 2019.

"Definition: Echo Chamber." *Cambridge Dictionary*. https://dictionary.cambridge.org/us/dictionary/english/echo-chamber. Accessed on October 21, 2019.

Franklin, C. "How Internet Search Engines Work." HowStuffWorks. N.D. https://computer.howstuffworks.com/internet/basics/search-engine.htm. Accessed on October 28, 2019.

Heshmat, S. "What Is Confirmation Bias?" *Psychology Today*. April 23, 2015. https://www.psychologytoday.com/us/blog/science-choice/201504/what-is-confirmation-bias. Accessed on October 21, 2019.

Mitchell, A. "Americans Still Prefer Watching to Reading the News—and Mostly Still through Television." Pew Research Center. December 3, 2018a. https://www.journalism.org/2018/12/03/americans-still-prefer-watching-to-reading-the-news-and-mostly-still-through-television/. Accessed on October 28, 2019.

Mitchell, A., et al. "Political Polarization & Media Habits." Pew Research Center. October 21, 2014. https://www.journalism.org/2014/10/21/political-polarization-media-habits/. Accessed on October 28, 2019.

"Sources and Search Engines." Code.org. N.D. https://curriculum.code.org/csd-1718/unit2/12/. Accessed on October 28, 2019.

"The Internet: How Search Works." Code.org. June 13, 2017. https://www.youtube.com/watch?v=LVV_93mBfSU. Accessed on October 28, 2019.

Websites

Bing. https://www.bing.com/. Accessed on October 25, 2019.

DuckDuckGo. https://duckduckgo.com/. Accessed on October 25, 2019.

Google. https://www.google.com/. Accessed on October 25, 2019.

Chapter 4 Activity

"Media Bias Chart 5.1." Ad Fontes Media. N.D. https://www.adfontesmedia.com/. Accessed on November 26, 2019.

Mitchell, A. "Americans Still Prefer Watching to Reading the News—and Mostly Still through Television." Pew Research Center: Journalism and Media. December 3, 2018b. https://www.journalism.org/2018/12/03/americans-still-prefer-watching-to-reading-the-news-and-mostly-still-through-television/. Accessed on November 26, 2019.

"Most Reliable and Credible Sources for Students." Common Sense Education. N.D. https://www.commonsense.org/education/top-picks/most-reliable-and-credible-sources-for-students. Accessed on November 26, 2019.

NPR Staff. "The Reason Your Feed Became an Echo Chamber — And What to Do About It." *All Tech Considered*. July 24, 2016. https://www.npr.org/sections/alltechconsidered/2016/07/24/486941582/the-reason-your-feed-became-an-echo-chamber-and-what-to-do-about-it. Accessed on November 26, 2019.

Sanger, L. "2013 : WHAT *SHOULD* WE BE WORRIED ABOUT?" *Edge*. N.D. https://www.edge.org/response-detail/23777. Accessed on November 26, 2019.

Shearer, E. and K.E. Matsa. "News Use across Social Media Platforms 2018." Pew Research Center: Journalism and Media. September 10, 2018. https://www.journalism.org/2018/09/10/news-use-across-social-media-platforms-2018/. Accessed on November 26, 2019.

5 Fact or Fiction?

There are a number of terms that are used to refer to incorrect information found on various forms of media. It's tough for adults to do the research necessary to ensure that they aren't taken in by inaccurate information, so it's no surprise that students struggle with this critical skill. This chapter lays the groundwork for educators to strengthen their own ability to differentiate between fact and fiction. It includes an activity readers and students can use to learn strategies designed to help them recognize one type of incorrect information called counterknowledge. Questions for reflection and a list of suggested resources complete the chapter.

Why Is This Important?

For better or worse, the words that people say, write, read, and hear influence their perceptions of the world—perhaps far more than we might think. For example, findings of an Australian study conducted in 2014 showed that misleading article headlines not only skewed readers' perceptions of what the article was about, but also impacted their later ability to accurately recall details about that article (Konnikova). If just a headline wields this much impact, imagine the damage that can be caused by full-blown media campaigns intentionally designed to mislead consumers.

Incorrect information in the media is referred to using several different terms. These commonly used terms are discussed in this chapter:

1. Misinformation: "incorrect or misleading information" ("Definition: Misinformation").
2. Disinformation: "a type of untrue communication that is purposefully spread and represented as truth to elicit some response that serves the perpetrator's purpose" ("Definition: Disinformation").
3. Counterknowledge: "misinformation packaged to look like fact" ("Definition: Counterknowledge").

The words misinformation and disinformation are often used interchangeably, but history writer and former magazine journalist Robert McNamara argues

Fact or Fiction? 27

that they do not mean the same thing in the strictest sense of the words. McNamara says that misinformation is spread innocently by someone who believes it to be true, whereas disinformation describes, "… an organized campaign to deceptively distribute untrue material intended to influence public opinion" (2019). Counterknowledge, a term coined by journalist Damien Thompson in 2008, enhances the meaning of disinformation by identifying specific examples such as unsubstantiated claims like those found in conspiracy theories (1).

A 2019 survey from Pew Research Center shows that the majority of Americans surveyed agree that the disinformation and counterknowledge currently found online and other media outlets significantly impact our country in a negative way. Furthermore, about one-half reported they have unknowingly passed along incorrect information they believed to be true when they shared it. Survey respondents also indicated that they think disinformation and counterknowledge create far more confusion than misinformation that was rushed to publication prior to fact-checking or that offers a slanted point of view (Mitchell et al.).

There are strategies consumers can use to fact-check information they find through various media outlets. A few are mentioned below in the Classroom Practice section of this chapter. Readers may also want to review Chapter 6, "Before You Share," for additional strategies. Finally, the activity for this chapter specifically addresses strategies for identifying examples of counterknowledge.

Real Life Examples

Misinformation, disinformation, and counterknowledge are nothing new. They have been around for centuries. For example, in 1769 John Adams and his cousin Sam helped a group of colonists fabricate and share stories they made up to turn public sentiment against the King (Parkinson). Even earlier, in 1279, the Hospitaliers of the Knights Templar surrendered a significant piece of property— a fort in Tripoli that had been granted more than a century earlier—when a group of Baibars who were laying siege to the fort presented them with a forged letter. Purportedly from the Grand Master of the Knights, the letter included directions telling the Hospitaliers to give the fort up to the Baibars (D'Costa). A major difference in modern times is the advent of numerous media outlets—e.g., print, radio, television, and the Internet—which make it ridiculously easy for anyone to distribute incorrect information around the world with almost no effort at all.

The impact of incorrect information ranges from relatively harmless to extremely disruptive. For example, it probably does not matter that people around the world were intentionally manipulated into believing a staged video allegedly depicting a pig rescuing a baby goat from a pond (Clarke). But then there was the young man who armed himself with an AR-15 semiautomatic rifle, a handgun, and a knife and then drove several hundred miles to a Washington, DC pizza joint. His self-proclaimed mission was to rescue children who—according to a conspiracy theory published widely online—were being held there by a group of pedophiles led by a candidate in the 2016 presidential election. Things got very serious very quickly. The man entered the crowded restaurant and fired one of his weapons at least once. Fortunately, no one was injured and he was quickly arrested. But the outcome could have been tragic (Robb). There are also multiple reports that since 2016, elections around the world have been meddled with by hackers based in Russia, China, and other locations. This is serious stuff.

Another example of counterknowledge is the deepfake. Prior to 2017, if a person watched a video of a public figure giving a speech, it was fairly easy to tell if it had been manipulated to make it appear that the speaker said or did something outrageous or out of character. Then, in late 2017, something called a deepfake was posted online. Tech Target defines this as "an AI-based technology used to produce or alter video content so that it presents something that didn't, in fact, occur." Although most of the early deepfakes were pornography, it wasn't long before people started using the technology to put words in the mouths of politicians and other public figures. In late 2018, CBC Kids News produced an episode that illustrated how easy it is to create a realistic deepfake (Resnick). Readers may view the deepfake created in that episode at https://www.cbc.ca/kidsnews/post/how-to-tell-if-a-viral-video-is-fake. Early deepfakes were still relatively easy to identify, but the artificial intelligence technology behind deepfakes is becoming increasingly sophisticated, making them more difficult to detect (Shao). This reality makes it even more critical that educators and students become more critical consumers of media.

Classroom Practice

In order to recognize misinformation, disinformation, and counterknowledge, students must be vigilant about vetting what they read, watch, and listen to. There are strategies educators can teach and then model to help students understand what they need to do to verify information and then be consistent in applying those strategies. It's also important to note that vetting information does not necessarily mean debunking everything checked. It can also mean confirming that something is true. It's necessary to make this distinction because one unanticipated consequence of disinformation and counterknowledge is that it can lead to consumers refusing to believe information that is true. Because so much of the material that requires vetting is related to news, the strategies presented here relate to fact-checking news. See the Classroom Practice section of Chapter 6 to see strategies for vetting other kinds of information.

MediaSmarts is a Canadian non-profit whose mission is to help students master effective media literacy skills. This organization suggests four strategies students and educators can employ to identify accurate news. They are presented here:

1. Avoid information echo chambers. As discussed in Chapter 4, expand the selection of news sources regularly accessed to read multiple perspectives about news. MediaSmarts recommends using AllSides (https://www.allsides.com/blog) which presents multiple perspectives about news events.

2. Use fact-checkers to verify information. Familiar fact-checkers include FactCheck.org (https://www.factcheck.org/) or Politifact (https://www.politifact.com/).
3. Share news responsibly. As discussed in Chapter 6, it's important to thinking before passing along news items or even discussing them online.
4. Report misinformation, disinformation, and counterknowledge whenever you come across it.

Another tool that is useful in recognizing media bias is the Interactive Media Bias Chart 5.0 (https://www.adfontesmedia.com/interactive-media-bias-chart/) from Ad Fontes Media. The chart depicts where various news sources fall on a continuum that ranges from most extreme left to most extreme right. Specific information about each news source is available.

As is the case with skills discussed in other chapters in this book, once students have received direct instruction in how to apply the strategies, they must be encouraged to use them on an ongoing basis.

Activity Plan

Activity: Counterknowledge—Journalist Damien Thompson defines counterknowledge as misinformation packaged to look like fact. It is manifested in multiple formats, including conspiracy theories, pseudoscience, and pseudohistory. It's tough for adults to do the research necessary to ensure that they aren't taken in by counterknowledge, so it's no surprise that students will struggle with sorting the wheat from the chaff.

What follows is a description of an activity readers may use themselves or with their students. The full activity plan including a student handout is available online in the Instructional Activities section at: http://medialiteracytoday.net. Please feel free to download the activity plan and handout files for ongoing use. This activity can be completed in one or two class sessions depending on the length of the instructional period and students' research skills.

Objective: Students work in teams to determine why the conspiracy theories presented to them are examples of counterknowledge (misinformation packaged to look like fact).

Standards: CCSS.ELA-LITERACY.RI.6.7-6.9, CCSS.ELA-LITERACY.SL.6.1-6.4, CCSS.ELA-LITERACY.W.6.7, CCSS.ELA-LITERACY.RI.7.8-7.9, CCSS.ELA-LITERACY.SL.7.1-7.4, CCSS.ELA-LITERACY.W.7.7, CCSS.ELA-LITERACY.RI.8.7-8.9, CCSS.ELA-LITERACY.SL.8.1-8.4, CCSS.ELA-LITERACY.W.8.7, CCSS.ELA-LITERACY.WHST.6-8.7

Outline—Set the Stage: Begin the activity by giving students a few minutes to consider what *counterknowledge* might mean and write down a few ideas. Then have students discuss their ideas with a shoulder partner. Share the definition—incorrect information packaged to look like fact—and ask students to write the definition in their own words. Mention that counterknowledge preys

30   *Fact or Fiction?*

on people's fears, often includes some elements of truth to make it seem plausible, and sometimes is the result of sensational news reporting.

Outline—Activity: Point out that counterknowledge may be presented in various ways, but one familiar format is the conspiracy theory. A conspiracy theory is defined by dictionary.com as "a theory that rejects the standard explanation for an event and instead credits a covert group or organization with carrying out a secret plot." There are many well-known conspiracy theories such as the moon landing was a hoax or the attack of 9/11 was the work of the US government. Lead a whole-class discussion in which you ask students to brainstorm a list of conspiracy theories familiar to them.

Explain that in this activity teams will research a well-known conspiracy theory to determine why that theory is an example of counterknowledge. In the course of this research students will:

- Consider the on- and offline sources they are using: Materials are provided for each conspiracy theory. Do these linked materials appear to be reliable sources? What can students do to determine reliability?
- Check the facts: Search online or review print reference materials to see if the event(s) described in the conspiracy theory happened as described. Try to find three reliable sources that confirm or deny the information presented as fact.
- Explain the conspiracy theory's structure including how it:
  - Targets people's fears or sense of insecurity
  - Weaves truth with fiction
  - Makes an interesting story

Walk the class through the Group Conspiracy Theory—JFK's Assassination in the **Counterknowledge Handout**. Ask them to read the description of the conspiracy theory and then model the three research steps presented in the Instruction portion of the lesson using on- and offline resources: consider the sources they are using; check the facts; and explain the structure of the conspiracy theory. Model the type of responses you expect to see on student handouts when they complete the rest of the activity independently. Assign a conspiracy theory to each team—there are just four so more than one team will research each theory.

Depending on your students' skill levels, you may decide to end the activity with the review of the JFK assassination conspiracy theory and then use some or all of the independent conspiracy theories in a center or as ongoing whole-group activities.

There are hundreds of examples of conspiracy theories. Based upon your students' interested and prior knowledge, you may decide to use a different example for the independent activity.

Outline—Extension: There are hundreds of conspiracy theories students can explore to further cement their abilities to identify the factors that make something like this appealing to people. Ask students to review the list they brainstormed earlier in this activity and select an additional conspiracy theory to explore.

Counterknowledge can also be presented as pseudoscience or pseudohistory. Ask students to define these terms and identify three to five examples of each.

Questions for Reflection

1. What are the most important ideas presented in this chapter, both for educators and for students?
2. How will you model the skills described in this chapter to ensure your students avoid being taken in by counterknowledge?
3. How can you structure learning activities to ensure that students have time to research and discuss examples of counterknowledge?
4. How will the information presented in this chapter impact your personal efforts to identify counterknowledge when you encounter an example?

Resources

Articles

Clarke, S. "Video of Pig Saving Baby Goat from Drowning Was Faked." *ABC News.* February 27, 2013. https://abcnews.go.com/blogs/headlines/2013/02/video-of-pig-saving-baby-goat-from-drowning-was-faked. Accessed on October 31, 2019.

D'Costa, K. "Three Historical Examples of 'Fake News'." *Scientific American.* December 1, 2016. https://blogs.scientificamerican.com/anthropology-in-practice/three-historical-examples-of-fake-news/. Accessed on November 1, 2019.

"Definition: Counterknowledge." Your Dictionary. https://www.yourdictionary.com/counterknowledge. Accessed on October 30, 2019.

"Definition: Deepfake." Tech Target. https://whatis.techtarget.com/definition/deepfake. Accessed on November 4, 2019.

"Definition: Disinformation." WhatIs.com. https://whatis.techtarget.com/definition/disinformation. Accessed on October 29, 2019.

"Definition: Misinformation." *Merriam-Webster.* https://www.merriam-webster.com/dictionary/misinformation. Accessed on October 30, 2019.

"Four Steps to Getting Better Political and Election News." MediaSmarts. N.D. http://mediasmarts.ca/digital-media-literacy/digital-issues/authenticating-information/impact-misinformation-democratic-process/four-steps-getting-better-political-election-news. Accessed on November 6, 2019.

Ireton, C. and J. Posetti. "Journalism, 'Fake News' & Disinformation." UNESCO Series on Journalism Education. 2018. https://en.unesco.org/sites/default/files/journalism_fake_news_disinformation_print_friendly_0.pdf. Accessed on October 29, 2019.

Isaac, M. "Dissent Erupts at Facebook over Hands-Off Stance on Political Ads. *New York Times.* October 28, 2019. https://www.nytimes.com/2019/10/28/technology/facebook-mark-zuckerberg-political-ads.html?module=inline&wpmm=1&wpisrc=nl_technology202. Accessed on October 29, 2019.

32 *Fact or Fiction?*

Konnikova, M. "How Headlines Change the Way We Think." *The New Yorker*. December 17, 2014. https://www.newyorker.com/science/maria-konnikova/headlines-change-way-think. Accessed on October 30, 2019.

McNamara, R. "What Is Disinformation? Definition and Examples." Thought.Co. March 25, 2019. https://www.thoughtco.com/disinformation-definition-4587093. Accessed on October 29, 2019.

Mitchell, A. et al. "Many Americans Say Made-Up News Is a Critical Problem That Needs To Be Fixed." Pew Research Center. June 5, 2019. https://www.journalism.org/2019/06/05/many-americans-say-made-up-news-is-a-critical-problem-that-needs-to-be-fixed/. Accessed on October 30, 2019.

Parkinson, R.G. "Fake News? That's a Very Old Story." *Washington Post*. November 25, 2016. https://www.washingtonpost.com/opinions/fake-news-thats-a-very-old-story/2016/11/25/c8b1f3d4-b330-11e6-8616-52b15787add0_story.html. Accessed on November 1, 2019.

"Political Disinformation." Media Smarts. N.D. http://mediasmarts.ca/digital-media-literacy/digital-issues/authenticating-information/impact-misinformation-democratic-process/political-disinformation. Accessed on October 29, 2019.

"Read the Letter Facebook Employees Sent to Mark Zuckerberg About Political Ads." *New York Times*. October 28, 2019. https://www.nytimes.com/2019/10/28/technology/facebook-mark-zuckerberg-letter.html?wpmm=1&wpisrc=nl_technology202. Accessed on October 29, 2019.

Resnick, A. "How to Tell If a Viral Video Is Fake." *CBC Kids News*. November 22, 2018. https://www.cbc.ca/kidsnews/post/how-to-tell-if-a-viral-video-is-fake. Accessed on November 4, 2019.

Robb, A. "Anatomy of a Fake News Scandal." Rolling Stone. November 16, 2017. https://www.rollingstone.com/politics/politics-news/anatomy-of-a-fake-news-scandal-125877/. Accessed on October 31, 2019.

Shao, G. "What 'Deepfakes' Are and How They May Be Dangerous." CNBC. October 13, 2019. https://www.cnbc.com/2019/10/14/what-is-deepfake-and-how-it-might-be-dangerous.html. Accessed on November 4, 2019.

Books

Thompson, D. *Counterknowledge*. New York: W. W. Norton & Company, 2008.

Chapter 5 Activity

"Hot Topics: Fake News and Misinformation: Identifying Fake News." University of Maine: Raymond H. Fogler Library. https://libguides.library.umaine.edu/fakenews/identification. Accessed on October 31, 2019.

Rogow, F. "Key Questions to Ask When Analyzing Media Messages." Project Look Sharp. 2017. https://www.projectlooksharp.org/Resources%202/keyquestions.pdf. Accessed on November 26, 2019.

6 Before You Share

Social media and other online platforms make it all too easy for users to "Like," "Share," "Tweet," or otherwise pass along misinformation or disinformation without intentionally becoming part of the counterknowledge problem. Studies say that students are actually better at identifying incorrect information than adults are, but they still do make mistakes. The activity for this chapter introduces strategies students and educators can use to verify items that appear in social media feeds and other media to ensure they are not passing along misinformation/disinformation. Questions for reflection and a list of suggested resources complete the chapter.

Why Is This Important?

People are subjected to a barrage of information every day. There is a lack of consistency in quality control associated with this information. Persons responsible for originally posting this information should be held accountable for its reliability, but that does not always happen. Therefore, it is increasingly important that media consumers take time to vet the truth of the items they read, watch, or listen to prior to passing them along to others. This does not shift all responsibility to the end consumer, nor should it, but it does remind consumers that they need to question information, not take it at face value.

As mentioned in Chapter 5, much of the disinformation people encounter is relatively harmless. Nuking a penny in a microwave will not cause the penny to shrink—although I'm not sure what might happen to the appliance (Evon). But even silliness like this may have an underlying purpose. If people can be convinced to distrust their own good judgment about something outlandish, but inconsequential in and of itself, does it becomes easier for them to do the same when they encounter disinformation related to serious matters?

Some experts also argue that current focus on "fake news" may give consumers the excuse to discount any information they disagree with solely on the belief that the media can't be trusted anyway (Weir). Rather than being a justification for not talking about disinformation and counterknowledge, I would argue this underscores the importance of educators teaching students the skills they need to be able to identify reliable information and to take the time to do

34 *Before You Share*

some fact-checking any time they are tempted to "Like," "Share," "Tweet," or otherwise disseminate information.

There is another factor to consider when thinking about why this matters. It's human nature to trust the people and organizations we know personally or by reputation over those we don't. If a well-informed colleague tags me on an article or video, or I read something from an organization I consider to be reliable, I am more likely to assume that the information is accurate than would be the case with an unknown source. Unfortunately, I understand that at the very time fact-checking is most needed, it simply isn't happening (Borel, 2). Again, this doesn't let media outlets off the hook—it is their responsibility to vet information before it's published. But even when these organizations are held accountable, it's up to consumers to double-check the information they encounter before passing it along to anyone else.

Real Life Examples

Examples of disinformation gone viral are plentiful. Fact-check websites like Snopes and Fact Checker host archives consisting of items that have been reviewed and rated for truthfulness. Snopes' collection of fact-checked items is organized by categories and found at https://www.snopes.com/archive/. (*Note*: Not all articles listed here are appropriate for student use.) FactCheck.org's archive is organized by a variety of categories including date, issue, people, and more. The majority of these are related to politics in some way. This archive is available at https://www.factcheck.org/archives/. Here are two examples of viral disinformation that resulted in negative consequences.

In 2012, as Hurricane Sandy bore down on the East Coast, a writer for *The Atlantic* invited readers to send him photos they saw online that were purportedly of the storm, but looked suspicious. He fact-checked the viral images that were sent and posted each image along with an explanation of whether it was real, fake, or unverified and why. This collection of photographs may be accessed at https://www.theatlantic.com/technology/archive/2012/10/sorting-the-real-sandy-photos-from-the-fakes/264243/ (Madrigal). But not everyone who posted online during or following the storm was trying to be helpful. A hedge fund analyst named Shashank Tripathi decided to make intentionally false posts. For example, he wrote that the New York Stock Exchange floor was flooded and that all electrical power to Manhattan was shut off. These statements were picked up by media outlets and reported as fact, adding to existing panic and confusion (Gross). The Manhattan District Attorney's office considered filing criminal charges against him and he lost his position as campaign manager for a Republican candidate for Congress.

When marijuana sales were legalized in Colorado as of January 1, 2014, it didn't take long before The National Report, a satirical website, posted a story claiming that a dispensary in Denver planned to accept food stamps (EBT cards) for purchases of marijuana-laced edibles. Despite the fact that the article was a spoof, several conservative online publications reported the spoof as fact (Bartles).

That following summer, a Republican state senator, Vicki Marble, began working on a bill to prohibit marijuana dispensaries from accepting food stamps based on her belief that the article was factual. That bill was not passed, but this example does demonstrate how easily disinformation can lead to wasting valuable resources to control non-existent behavior based on an urban myth.

It's important to note that Internet trolls, and bots—autonomous programs that spread information that is often inaccurate and designed to influence readers' opinions about various topics—are regularly used to initiate online disinformation campaigns. However, it's everyday people who end up fanning the flames that make an article go viral. Avoid becoming part of one of these campaigns by sharing carefully.

Classroom Practice

The activity for this chapter focuses on basic fact-checking strategies educators and students can use whenever they are thinking about liking or reposting information they encounter online. In addition to those general tips, there are some activities you can use yourself and with students to practice and expand fact-checking skills.

Never underestimate the value of practice. Despite the fact you will review tips within the context of an activity, we all need to use the skills associated with those recommendations on a regular basis or our fact-checking skills will rapidly decline. One strategy for encouraging ongoing fact-checking is to make it a regular part of assignments. Require evidence of fact-checking in whatever students turn in for grading. It may be as simple as a checklist or more complex—perhaps requiring students to document resources used during fact-checking. This serves two purposes. First, it reminds students how important fact-checking actually is and it helps them keep their skills sharp. The more checking they do, the better and faster they will be at the task.

Another general strategy is to take advantage of pre-existing online games and other activities based on fact-checking. Here are some to review:

1. Many people can't tell when photos are fake. Can you? (https://www.washingtonpost.com/news/speaking-of-science/wp/2017/07/17/many-people-cant-tell-when-photos-are-fake-can-you/): This article from the *Washington Post* features a link to a quiz (https://www.washingtonpost.com/can-you-tell-fake-news-when-you-see-it/54143932-efb7-46de-af6b-f92108a329dc_quiz.html) that challenges students to identify photographs that have been digitally altered.
2. News Lit Quiz: Real or Not? (https://newslit.org/get-smart/which-is-legit/): News Literacy Project created this quiz to challenge students to determine if a news source is legitimate or not. Instead of guessing, ask students to research each outlet before making decisions.
3. NewsFeed Defenders (https://www.factcheck.org/newsfeed-defenders/): Hosted by FactCheck.org, this web-based game challenges students to

36 *Before You Share*

fact-check a series of social media posts. A free lesson plan and other support materials are available for teachers who sign up for an account. The target audience is high school, but middle school students can complete the activity in teams or as a whole class activity.

A fact-checking technique that may be new to educators and students is a Google reverse image search which can be used to check the validity of online images. Go to images.google.com. Click on the camera icon. Conduct the actual search by pasting in the URL of an image found on the web, upload an image, or drag an image from another open window. If using the Chrome browser, it's also possible to right-click on any image to immediately generate a search. The results show where the image can be found online which helps users determine if the image is actually what it is claimed to be, if it has been manipulated in some way, or if it is being used out of context. Challenge students to research the origins of online images using this simple technique.

Activity Plan

Activity: Before You Share—Social media platforms make it all too easy for users to "Like," "Share," "Tweet," or otherwise pass along misinformation or disinformation without intentionally becoming part of the counterknowledge problem. Anyone who has one or more social media accounts needs to take the time to verify that articles, memes, photographs, and anything else they pass along to their friends are based in fact. Studies say that students are actually better at identifying incorrect information than adults are, but they still do make mistakes.

What follows is a description of an activity readers may use themselves or with their students. The full activity plan, including a student handout, is available online in the Instructional Activities section at: http://medialiteracytoday. net. Please feel free to download the activity plan and handout files for ongoing use. This activity can be completed in one or two class sessions depending on the length of the instructional period and students' research skills.

Objective: Students work in teams to apply tips they learn during the activity to verify online items which may, or may not, be true prior to sharing them with anyone else.

Standards: CCSS.ELA-LITERACY.RI.6.7-6.9, CCSS.ELA-LITERACY. SL.6.1-6.4, CCSS.ELA-LITERACY.W.6.7, CCSS.ELA-LITERACY.RI.7.8-7.9, CCSS.ELA-LITERACY.SL.7.1-7.4, CCSS.ELA-LITERACY.W.7.7, CCSS. ELA-LITERACY.RI.8.7-8.9, CCSS.ELA-LITERACY.SL.8.1-8.4, CCSS.ELA-LITERACY.W.8.7, CCSS.ELA-LITERACY.WHST.6-8.7

Outline—Set the Stage: Open the activity by giving students 5–10 minutes to discuss the following questions in their teams:

1. Why is it important to verify the truthfulness of articles, photos, memes, or other digital material before posting them online?

Before You Share 37

2. Is it as important to check these same items if someone they follow online first posts it and they are simply reposting or liking it?
3. Does it make a difference when an item is posted by someone they actually know—a friend or family member?

Following a brief class discussion about their responses to the questions, mention that most people feel comfortable reposting items their friends and family members have posted without checking these items as carefully as they might otherwise. Say that this is one way misinformation spreads quickly online.

Outline—Activity: Ask students which social media platforms they currently use. Make a list of these tools and query students in general terms about why they use these particular platforms, who they friend or follow, who friends and follows them, and how digital materials are shared. Ask how people indicate they approve of something someone else has posted. Is there a way to like something? To repost something or make a comment on it? Ask if they carefully read and check out items they react to or if they blindly give their approval. If the latter, why? Remind them that social media and other platforms are hotbeds of counterknowledge because it's so easy to pass misinformation along with a click or tap.

Give students a few minutes to brainstorm and list strategies they already use to check online materials before passing them along to others. Share and discuss the following tips with the class.

1. Read the post and material that may be linked. In the case of a photo, look at it closely.
2. Check the source. Is the information published by a known, reliable person or institution?
3. Search to see who else is posting about this event or topic. Are those sources reliable?
4. Is the title or headline sensational? Does it accurately reflect the rest of the content?
5. Does the text, meme, or image seem to be too good to be true or is it designed to stir your emotions?
6. Use a fact-checker like Snopes.com or FactCheck. Has the information already been evaluated by one or more of these sites?

Ask students to identify five tips they will use as they complete this activity.

Give students main ideas for four actual articles, four examples of online memes, and four photographs. The online materials developed for this activity provide everything needed to complete the assignment or teachers may want to gather their own examples.

Depending on your students' skill levels and available time, you may decide to have teams work on just one of the exercises (articles, memes, or photographs) and then share answers in the class discussion.

38   *Before You Share*

Outline—Extension: There are hundreds of examples of articles, memes, and photographs that are said to be true but aren't or that seem to be untrue, but are actually true. Ask students to be aware of these and bring examples to class.

There are also examples of videos that have been edited to change viewers' perceptions of truth. Students might be interested in researching deepfake videos to demonstrate this.

Questions for Reflection

1.   What are the most important ideas presented in this chapter, both for educators and for students?
2.   How will you model the skills described in this chapter to ensure your students recognize the importance of fact-checking prior to sharing information they see online?
3.   How can you structure learning activities to ensure that students take time to fact-check?
4.   How will the information presented in this chapter impact your personal efforts to fact-check prior to passing along information that has turned up in your social media feeds?

Resources

Articles

Bartles, L. "Fake Report about Colorado Pot Shops, Food Stamps Creates Havoc." *The Denver Post.* Updated April 27, 2016. https://www.denverpost.com/2014/01/14/fake-report-about-colorado-pot-shops-food-stamps-creates-havoc/. Accessed on November 14, 2019.

"Colorado Pot Shop Accepting Food Stamps – Taxpayer Funded Marijuana for Welfare Recipients." Snopes. 2014. https://www.snopes.com/fact-check/brownie-points/. Accessed on July 22, 2020.

Evon, D. "Will Putting a Penny in a Microwave Cause the Coin to Shrink?" Snopes. November 11, 2019. https://www.snopes.com/fact-check/shrink-a-penny-in-a-microwave/. Accessed on November 14, 2019.

Gross, D. "Man faces fallout for spreading false Sandy reports on Twitter." CNN. October 31, 2012. https://www.cnn.com/2012/10/31/tech/social-media/sandy-twitter-hoax/index.html. Accessed on July 22, 2020.

Madrigal, A.C. "Sorting the Real Sandy Photos from the Fakes." *The Atlantic.* October 29, 2012. https://www.theatlantic.com/technology/archive/2012/10/sorting-the-real-sandy-photos-from-the-fakes/264243/. Accessed on November 14, 2019.

"News Lit Quiz: How news-literate are you?" News Literacy Project. https://newslit.org/get-smart/how-news-literate-are-you-quiz/. Accessed on July 22, 2020.

"NewsFeed Defenders." FactCheck.org. 2019. https://www.factcheck.org/newsfeed-defenders/ Accessed on November 16, 2019.

"The International Fact-Checking Network." Poynter. https://www.poynter.org/ifcn/. Accessed on November 7, 2019.

Wan, W. "Many People Can't Tell When Photos Are Fake. Can You?" *The Washington Post.* July 17, 2017. https://www.washingtonpost.com/news/speaking-of-science/wp/2017/07/17/many-people-cant-tell-when-photos-are-fake-can-you/. Accessed on November 16, 2019.

Weir, K. "Why We Believe Alternative Facts." *American Psychological Association 48*(5): 24, May 2017. https://www.apa.org/monitor/2017/05/alternative-facts. Accessed on November 14, 2019.

Books

Borel, B. *The Chicago Guide to Fact-Checking.* Chicago, IL: University of Chicago Press, 2016.

Chapter 6 Activity

FactCheck.org. The Annenberg Public Policy Center. https://www.factcheck.org/. Accessed on November 26, 2019.

Kessler, G. "Washington Post Fact Checker." *Washington Post.* https://www.washingtonpost.com/news/fact-checker/. Accessed on November 26, 2019.

Politifact. The Poynter Institute. https://www.politifact.com/. Accessed on November 26, 2019.

Slayer, H. and Christensen, B.M.. https://www.hoax-slayer.net/. Accessed on November 26, 2019.

Snopes, Snopes Media Group. https://www.snopes.com/. Accessed on November 26, 2019.

7   Can You Believe That?

People frequently use statistics to lend credence to a point: however, numbers don't necessarily denote facts. Misrepresented numbers give false impressions that may be entirely meaningless. A simple check of the validity of a statistic is to ask how believable it is. This test requires nothing more than common sense and rudimentary math skills to determine the plausibility of any claim (Levitin). The activity for this chapter offers strategies educators and students can use when they encounter claims supported by statistics in the media to determine if they are plausible. Questions for reflection and a list of suggested resources completes the chapter.

Why Is This Important?

Cambridge Dictionary defines *plausible* as: "possibly true; able to be believed." As mentioned above, numbers are often used to justify claims. These numbers may be in the form of raw data, averages, survey results, data visualizations, or something else. How closely do you review numbers you read, see, or hear about, or do you assume that the writer or speaker's work is fact-checked and verified prior to being put out for public consumption, therefore making it plausible? At one time, that assumption may have had some validity, but in today's environment of the citizen journalist, where people turn to amateur reporters' posts on social media for their news, it's more imperative than ever to ask how plausible the numbers actually are.

What is citizenship journalism? Techopedia defines citizenship journalism as "… the reporting of news events by members of the public using the Internet to spread the information." A citizen journalist may take on tasks as mundane as reporting on local sports programs or reviewing restaurants around town. They may also opt to tackle critical local, state, federal, even international concerns. Their reporting typically appears on social media platforms, websites, podcasts, and video sites—pretty much anywhere a person can upload digital material (Rogers).

When citizenship journalism was first recognized as being a "thing," people were excited about the possibilities. For example, the Federal Emergency Management Agency (FEMA) reported in 2013 that during and after Hurricane Sandy, "users sent more than 20 million Sandy-related Twitter posts, or 'tweets,' despite the loss of cell phone service during the peak of the storm" (Maron). Many of those Tweets did include important information about the storm, but initial enthusiasm waned quickly. In the wake of the 2013 Boston Marathon bombing, the Boston Police Department used social media to inform the local community and the world about what was happening, but also spent a great deal of time correcting misinformation that citizen journalists were posting online (Walker).

Numbers are regularly distorted by amateurs and professionals alike, both inadvertently and intentionally. In the end, it is up to consumers to question the statistics and data visualizations they come across. Fortunately, common sense goes a long way when initially checking numbers. Chapters 8 through 11 address strategies for examining numbers in various specific ways such as understanding averages, reviewing data collection techniques, taking a closer look at data visualizations, and probability. This chapter provides tips for making initial broad assessments of numbers cited in articles, television or radio broadcasts, and more.

Real Life Examples

The examples provided here offers suggestions for checking the plausibility of numbers in three common situations: misleading data visualization; misleading claims; and misleading correlations.

Misleading data visualizations: Let's begin with data visualizations such as graphs. Media outlets rely heavily on pictorial depictions of data because they condense a lot of information into a format that is easy to read and understand. The challenge is that data visualizations are also easy to distort. Consumers will want to look carefully at data visualizations to ensure what they are viewing is accurate, but many are blatantly out of whack and can be identified and discarded quickly.

Consumers don't need to be statisticians to know that the segments of a pie chart must add up to 100% or that the y-axis (vertical axis) starts with "0" at the bottom and then increases in constant increments going up. There are times when the y-axis might legitimately start with a number greater than "0," but at a cursory first look, consumers need to note when that number is something other than "0" and how that might impact the information being presented.

This will be discussed in greater depth in Chapter 10. Other items to note quickly include presence or absence of a title and labels or use of disproportionate images or icons rather than lines or bars to represent data size. A quick Internet search using the keywords "incorrect graphs" results in millions of examples consumers can use to familiarize themselves with what to look for.

Misleading claims: These are statements that often include numeric "evidence," but are not true. For example, a few years ago the manufacturer of a sugary breakfast cereal marketed to children claimed that children who ate one bowl of this cereal in the morning increased their attentiveness by 20%. Who wouldn't want their child to be more attentive, right? But common sense and personal experience should tell anyone that the statement is ridiculous and the mention

42 *Can You Believe That?*

of a percentage ought to lead consumers to ask how something like that would be measured. A judge agreed and the company was required to set up a fund to reimburse customers who purchased the cereal.

Suppose a politician claimed that the number of opioid addicts in West Virginia has doubled every year since 1990. Does that seem reasonable? Taken at face value it might, but do the math. Assume there was one opioid addict in the state in 1988 and work the problem from there. How many addicts are there by 2018? Keep in mind that the population of the entire state was 1.806 million in 2018. If the number of addicts did double annually, in 20 years (2008), a decade later there would have been 2,097,152 people living in West Virginia who were addicted to opioids—more than the entire population of the state!

It's important to avoid accepting any statistics presented at face value.

Misleading Correlations and Causation: People make sense of the world by looking for patterns. *Correlation* is defined by Dictionary.com as being a "mutual relation of two or more things, parts, etc." In other words, a kind of pattern. For example, people get thirsty when they are dehydrated or gasoline prices increase around major holidays. In each case, there is a relationship between the two things. But not all correlations make sense. In his book *Spurious Correlations*, Tyler Vigen explains that given enough data to dig through, it's possible to identify patterns that don't actually correlate, even when it seems they do. The technique used to do this is called data dredging. It involves using a computer to compare one variable against hundreds of other unrelated variables until a pattern is detected. The problem is that the pattern is meaningless. One well-known example Vigen cites is the data-dredged correlation between the number of Nicholas Cage movies made in any given year and the number of people who fall into swimming pools and drown in the same year. There does appear to be a pattern, but of course it is just a coincidence (Vigen, xi–xii).

A further concern is that people often assume that every correlation implies something called *causation*, which Merriam-Webster defines as "the act or process of causing something to happen or exist." In the examples given previously, people get thirsty because they are dehydrated or gasoline prices increase because a holiday is happening soon. These are examples of correlation and causation. But do people really fall into swimming pools and drown because Nicolas Cage appears in a film? Not likely. Common sense and a basic understanding of data dredging are useful in recognizing spurious correlations.

Classroom Practice

When it comes to determining plausibility, the most important mathematics concept to rely on is *number sense*. Educator Jennifer Hogan defines number sense as "… a person's ability to understand, relate, and connect numbers." She elaborates by listing four indicators of good number sense which include the ability to:

- Visualize and talk comfortably about numbers.
- Take numbers apart and put them back together in different ways.

- Compute mentally.
- Relate numbers to real-life problems by connecting them to their everyday world.

(Hogan)

These are precisely the skills educators need to foster in their students to help them determine the plausibility of numbers they encounter in the media. But what strategies can educators adopt to help students become more proficient in these skills? It's essential that these skills be extended beyond math instruction. Students deal with numbers throughout the day. They need to be encouraged to think about them within the context of the real world. Educators need to be sure they model these skills, pointing out what they are doing and why. Developing number sense isn't a one and done learning experience. This concept needs to be incorporated into learning activities whenever possible.

Here are a few suggestions for practices that will help students regularly practice skills related to number sense.

1. Mental math: When students make calculations in their heads, they are strengthening their understanding of numbers and numeric relationships. This understanding makes it easier for them to determine if numbers they are vetting are plausible.
2. Estimate: Think about the ways people commonly use math day-to-day. Mental math and estimation are frequently coupled as questions like:

   a. How long will it take to complete this task?
   b. How much will a new backpack cost?
   c. What is the distance from point A to point B?

   There are numerous opportunities to ask students to practice these skills by making estimations throughout the day.
3. Multiple problem-solving strategies: The days of insisting that students solve problems using a specified strategy are gone. Nearly any problem can be solved using more than one approach. Encourage students to broaden their thinking by trying and sharing multiple approaches. This practice can range from academic exercises like working a math problem to real life situations like streamlining classroom procedures.
4. Thinking out loud: Ask students to verbalize their thinking processes while they are solving problems. If desirable, ask them to capture that thinking using an audio or video recorder on a phone or tablet to upload to secure cloud storage for later review. This practice helps students think about their thinking and gives educators a window on students' thought processes.

Students can also practice recognizing numeric plausibility by adopting an approach used by fact-checkers when reading information that includes numerical data. Begin by highlighting every number that is mentioned. Based on what

44 *Can You Believe That?*

they know (or think they know) about the topic, students can predict which numbers are accurate and which are not. Have them conduct research to locate reliable primary sources that confirm the accuracy of the numbers. Which are easiest to verify? Which are more difficult to track down? Why? Engage students in discussions about their findings. The purpose of this exercise is to encourage students to take time to think whenever they read material that includes numbers (Borel).

Activity Plan

Activity: People frequently use statistics to lend credence to a point: however, numbers don't necessarily denote facts. Misrepresented numbers give false impressions that may be entirely meaningless. A simple check of the validity of a statistic is to ask how believable it is. This test requires nothing more than common sense and rudimentary math skills to determine the plausibility of any claim.

What follows is a description of an activity readers may use themselves or with their students. The full activity plan, including a student handout, is available online in the Instructional Activities section at: http://medialiteracytoday. net. Please feel free to download the activity plan and handout files for ongoing use. This activity can be completed in one or two class sessions depending on the length of the instructional period and students' research skills.

Objective: Students work in teams to review multiple claims that are supported by statistics and decide if those claims are plausible.

Standards: CCSS.MATH.PRACTICE.MP3, Grades 6–8

Outline—Set the Stage: Open the activity by asking students the following questions:

1. What does the word *statistics* mean? (A definition is provided on the Activity Preparation page for this activity.)
2. Are statistics facts? (No, statistics are interpretations, they are not facts.)
3. Are statistics that are presented in an article or media report generally accurate? (Not necessarily. Informed media consumers know they need to check statistics they read or hear to determine if they are believable.)
4. What does the word *plausible* mean? (A definition is provided on the Activity Preparation page for this activity.)

Students then engage in a K-W-L activity about how statistics are used in media.

Outline—Activity: Explain that student teams will review multiple claims that use statistics to prove a point and decide if these claims are plausible.

Review these five questions (provided at the top of the handout available online):

1. What is the claim?
2. Do you think the claim is plausible or believable?
3. What information do you need to check?

4. What reliable resources (at least two) did you find that validate the information you are checking or what mathematical calculations did you make to check the information?
5. What did you learn about the plausibility/believability of this claim?

Walk students through the first three questions using an example claim found on the handout or provide your own. Lead a brainstorming session on strategies students can use to find answers to questions 4 and 5, then give them time to do the research. Check students' responses prior to asking them to respond to the five claims provided on the handout.

Possible Modification: If necessary, walk through verifying the claims as a whole-class activity. You may also assign one or two claims to each team instead of all five.

Outline—Extension: There are hundreds of examples of print, video, and audio stories that use statistics to make a case for something. Ask students to be aware of these and bring examples to class.

Questions for Reflection

1. What are the most important ideas presented in this chapter, both for educators and for students?
2. How will you model the skills described in this chapter to ensure your students recognize the importance of determining if statistics used to support claims are plausible?
3. How can you structure learning activities to ensure that students take time to verify the statistics?
4. How will the information presented in this chapter impact your personal efforts to determine if statistics used to support claims are plausible?

Resources

Articles

"Definition: Causation." *Merriam-Webster.* https://www.merriam-webster.com/dictionary/causation. Accessed on November 27, 2019.

"Definition: Citizen Journalism." techopedia. https://www.techopedia.com/definition/2386/citizen-journalism. Accessed on November 26, 2019.

"Definition: Correlation." Dictionary.com. https://www.dictionary.com/browse/correlation. Accessed on November 27, 2019.

"Definition: Plausible." *Cambridge Dictionary.* https://dictionary.cambridge.org/us/dictionary/english/plausible. Accessed on November 27, 2019.

Hogan, J. "Demystifying Math: What Is Number Sense?" Scholastic Parents. https://www.scholastic.com/parents/school-success/learning-toolkit-blog/demystifying-math-what-number-sense.html. Accessed on November 28, 2019.

Maron, D.F. "How Social Media Is Changing Disaster Response." *Scientific American.* June 7, 2013. https://www.scientificamerican.com/article/how-social-media-is-changing-disaster-response/. Accessed on November 26, 2019.

46   *Can You Believe That?*

Newcombe, T. "Social Media: Big Lessons from the Boston Marathon Bombing." Government Technology. September 24, 2014. https://www.govtech.com/public-safety/Social-Media-Big-Lessons-from-the-Boston-Marathon-Bombing.html. Accessed on November 26, 2019.

Rogers, T. "Understanding Citizen Journalism." ThoughtCo. Updated January 15, 2019. https://www.thoughtco.com/what-is-citizen-journalism-2073663.   Accessed   on November 25, 2019.

Walker, P. "Boston Bombing Identification Attempts on Social Media End in Farce." *The Guardian.* April 19, 2013. https://www.theguardian.com/world/2013/apr/19/boston-bombing-suspects-reddit-social-media. Accessed on November 26, 2019.

Books

Borel, B. *The Chicago Guide to Fact-Checking.* Chicago, IL: University of Chicago Press 2016.

Levitin, D.J. *Weaponized Lies: How to Think Critically in the Post-Truth Era.* New York: Dutton 2017.

Vigen, T. *Spurious Correlations: Correlation Does Not Equal Correlation.* New York: Hachette Books 2015.

Chapter 7 Activity

Brown, A. "How We Check Numbers and Facts at Pew Research Center." *Opinion Today.* August 14, 2019. https://opiniontoday.com/2019/08/14/how-we-check-numbers-and-facts-at-pew-research-center/. Accessed on November 29, 2019.

FactCheck.org. The Annenberg Public Policy Center. https://www.factcheck.org/. Accessed on November 29, 2019.

"Primary Sources." Wayne State University Library System. https://guides.lib.wayne.edu/PrimarySources. Accessed on November 29, 2019.

"What's a Primary Resource?" University of Wyoming Libraries. July 30, 2018. https://uwyo.libguides.com/c.php?g=97853&p=632756. Accessed on November 29, 2019.

8 Those Pesky Averages

The nice thing about averages is they reduce a lot of numbers down to one. The challenge with averages is they can be calculated in at least three different ways—and that one number reported may not represent what people think unless they know to ask if they are looking at the mean, median, mode, or some other type of average and why that particular one was chosen. This chapter walks educators through a quick review of how the three most common types of averages are calculated and tips for recognizing when they are misrepresented. The activity for this chapter offers opportunities to review multiple examples of claims supported by averages to decide if those averages represent truthful information. Questions for reflection and a list of suggested resources completes the chapter.

Why Is This Important?

People deal with massive amounts of information every day. Any strategy that can be used to condense a lot of data into simple, easy-to-digest bits is welcomed by most consumers. There is value in making information more accessible to end users. However, if doing that creates misunderstandings about what the data represent or how to interpret what's being reported, it's just swapped one problem for another. The concept of averages is introduced to students as young as Grade 3, making it an idea most people are familiar with to some degree. They have a basic understanding of how to calculate the *mean* average of a set of numbers and what that number represents, but may not clearly remember how to identify the *median* or *mode* for that data set or why they might want to do that. And why would they?

Most of the time when people run across averages in the media, the mean is what's being discussed. But there are times when that isn't the case. This is why it's important that educators ensure their students understand the three main

48 *Those Pesky Averages*

types of averages, how they are calculated and when each type is typically used. Here's a quick review of how to calculate each.

- Mean—Add up all the numbers in a given data set and divide by the number of numbers in the set. Example: 9, 14, 14, 15, 16, 16, 19, 21, 21, 21, 21

$$\left(9+14+14+15+16+16+19+21+21+21+21\right)\div 11 = 17$$

- Median—The middle number in a data set. List all the numbers in the series from lowest to highest. The median in the example above is 16.
- Mode—The number in a data set that is repeated most often. The mode in the example is 21. If no number in the series is repeated, there is no mode (Purplemath).

When should the different kinds of averages be used? Here is a brief overview for each.

- Mean—Use the mean when the data set does not include outliers, numbers that are exceptionally lower or higher than the other numbers in the series. Also, do not use the mean when the data set represents results of a survey where respondents have been asked to indicate preference about something. For example, to rate something on a scale of 1–5 (University of Leicester).
- Median—Use the median when the data set does include outliers because these high or low numbers have less impact on the outcome in this case. Also, the median is a better way to represent the average when dealing with numbers used to indicate a preference—ranking on a scale of 1–5, for example (University of Leicester).
- Mode—The mode comes in handy when it's important to report categorical data in terms of which was most popular. For instance, if the data set given above represents the highest number of dollars office workers are willing to pay for lunch, the mode is 21 because it is the number that appears most often in the data set. This could be significant information for the owner of a local restaurant, but it's also important to note that this number is higher than what the overall data represents. In addition, some data sets have no mode at all, while others may have two or more modes (University of Leicester).

Let's take a look a few examples of how averages can be manipulated to misinform consumers.

Real Life Examples

It probably comes as no surprise that in the real world averages are often misused—sometimes intentionally, but not always. Here are three examples of how this happens.

Those Pesky Averages 49

Example 1: A young couple is looking for an apartment in a neighborhood they both like. The highest monthly payment they can afford is $1850. They speak with a property manager who tells them that the average monthly rent in that neighborhood is $2011.11, which is $161.11 more than they can afford. He shows them a list of monthly charges for nine recent rentals:

1575, 1650, 1650, 1800, 1800, 1875, 2000, 2750, 3000

As they review his figures, the couple sees that while the property manager has given them the mean average for rental apartments, the median for rents is actually $1800 which is within their budget and better reflects rental fees in general in that neighborhood than the mean, which is skewed by the top rental fees, which are quite a bit higher than the rest.

Example 2: A family is researching local high schools for their daughter to attend in the fall. They are particularly interested in schools' track records for the number of graduates that are admitted to 4-year colleges. A counselor at one high school they are considering provides a fact sheet stating that:

The average number of seniors graduating each year over the previous nine years = 581.11

The average number of graduates admitted to college each year = 443.22

The parents note that the college admittance average does not specifically mention 4-year colleges. The counselor agrees to find out if that number represents all college admissions or just 4-year college admissions. He contacts the parents a few days later to say that the averages originally presented represent students admitted to both 2-year and 4-year colleges. In reality, the average number of graduates admitted to 4-year colleges is 159.33. In other words, the majority of seniors who are admitted to college on graduation are going to 2-year colleges. Follow-up data on which students complete 2-year programs and then go on to 4-year colleges are not available. This additional information may or may not be important in the long run, but it does provide more accurate information about the school. In this example, the data are misleading because the family wanted to look at a specific subgroup of students but were shown overall information instead.

Example 3: This last example looks at test grades for two subgroups of 11 students each in one class period. In the first group, 1 student scored 70 on the test, 2 students scored 75, 4 scored 80, 1 scored 85, 1 scored 90, and 2 scored 100. In the second group, 1 student scored 50 on the test, 3 scored 70, 3 scored 85, and 4 scored 100. The mean test score for each group is 83.18, but did both groups actually perform at the same level? The median score for Group 1 is 80 and the median score for Group 2 is 85. The mode for Group 1 is 80 and the mode for Group 2 is 100. Do either of these averages give a more accurate picture of each group's performance on that test?

50 *Those Pesky Averages*

Classroom Practice

Beginning in Grade 6 students start using what they have learned about numbers to make sense of statistics (Common Core State Standards Initiative). In the case of averages, students have learned how to calculate mean, median, and mode, and are ready to explore what the different averages represent as well as how they can be used or misused when reporting data. This requires time and ongoing practice. Then once students achieve understanding, educators need to ensure they don't give students permission to forget what they've learned.

What do I mean by the phrase "permission to forget?" It's not unusual to provide instruction in an important concept, assess students' mastery of the material, and move on to the next topic without ever revisiting previously taught material until the end of the semester or school year when the information pops up again on a comprehensive exam or standardized test. In effect, students get the message that what they've learned was important in the short term, but now it's time to tuck that information away somewhere and move on to something else. Yes, educators are expected to cover massive amounts of information in almost every course, and it's not realistic to think that every concept can be retaught over and over. However, it is possible to use regularly scheduled activities that allow students to review material already taught. Let's think about how this might be accomplished when working with averages.

In the case of averages, students need to remember how to calculate them. They also need opportunities to think about what the different averages represent and how they can be used to inform others. There are various strategies educators employ that can emphasize review. For example:

- Daily "sponge" activities students complete as they enter the classroom and are waiting for class to begin.
- "Exit tickets" completed at the end of the class period.
- Learning centers used by students on a daily or weekly basis.

These are all occasional—but regularly scheduled—activities that can happen at predetermined intervals.

How might this work with averages? Brainstorm a list of real classroom data students can use. We collect all kinds of data like test scores, assignment statistics, or monthly attendance in which sets of numbers can be presented to students with no specifically identifying information included. Newspapers, print or digital, are another source of data such as weather, sports, or the stock market. Students can generate their own data by creating and/or responding to short surveys and then analyzing the results. There are also online data sets that can be accessed and used for analysis, for example, Data.Gov. Or, check out the list of free data set sites included in T.J. DeGroat's article, "19 Free Public Data Sets for Your Data Science Project," referenced in the Resources section below.

Commit to having students continue to work with averages weekly or monthly. Challenge them to work with authentic data. Include activities that ask them to calculate mean, median, and mode, but then also to do something with the results. These activities can also be tied to math concepts covered in Chapters 9 through 11 in this book, making it possible to broaden the impact of the review activities. For instance, Chapter 10 focuses on data visualizations. Once averages have been calculated and analyzed, students can create graphs designed to inform (or misinform).

An important piece of these activities is giving students permission to explore not just accurate use of the data, but also its misuse. Students need to have direct experience with intentional creation of misinformation to be able to know what to look for as they consume information.

Activity Plan

Activity: Mean, Median, and Mode—The nice thing about averages is they reduce a lot of numbers down to one. The challenge with averages is they can be calculated in at least three different ways—and that the number reported may not represent what people think unless they know to ask if they are looking at the mean, median, mode, or some other type of average and why that particular one was chosen.

What follows is a description of an activity readers may use themselves or with their students. The full activity plan including a student handout is available online in the Instructional Activities section at: http://medialiteracytoday.net. Please feel free to download the activity plan and handout files for ongoing use. This activity can be completed in one or two class sessions depending on the length of the instructional period and students' research skills.

Objective: Students work in teams to review how to calculate mean, median, and mode for a series of numbers and then explore ways that claims supported by averages can be reported to give readers a false impression about what the numbers mean.

Standards: CCSS.MATH.PRACTICE.MP3, Grades 6–8

Outline—Set the Stage: Open the activity by asking students to independently write their own definitions for the terms: *mean, median,* and *mode.* Allow them to use on- or offline resources, if needed.

Then give them time to talk with members of their teams to compare their definitions and correct any mistakes.

Outline—Activity: Tell students that the nice thing about averages is they reduce a lot of numbers down to one, but that the challenge with averages is they can be calculated in three different ways. Mention that the number reported may not represent what people think unless they know to ask if they are looking at the mean, median, or mode.

Use the example scenario provided in the handout (or create one of your own) to walk students through individually calculating the mean, median, and mode for the data set provided and then work as a team to answer the four questions about how those averages could be used to give false impressions about what the data mean.

52 *Those Pesky Averages*

Check students' responses to the example scenario. Give teams time to work through the remaining three scenarios included in the handout (or create your own).

Possible Modification: Depending on your students' skill levels and available time, you may decide to have teams work on just one of the scenarios (assign one scenario to each team) and then share answers in the class discussion.

Outline—Extension: Challenge students to create their own scenarios, data sets, and questions to share with one another. This will help them think more deeply about the concepts in this activity and will also provide all class members additional practice in recognizing when averages are being used selectively to give different impressions about the meaning of a data set. Students may want to review news articles for ideas they can use to develop their scenarios.

Questions for Reflection

1. What are the most important ideas presented in this chapter, both for educators and for students?
2. How will you model the skills described in this chapter to ensure your students recognize the importance of understanding how averages can be reported to give readers a false impression about what the numbers mean?
3. How can you structure learning activities to ensure that students take time to verify averages when presented?
4. How will the information presented in this chapter impact your personal efforts to understand how averages can be reported to give readers a false impression about what the numbers mean?

Resources

Articles

DeGroat, T.J. "19 Free Public Data Sets for Your Data Science Project." Springboard Blog. August 21, 2018. https://www.springboard.com/blog/free-public-data-sets-data-science-project/. Accessed on December 7, 2019.

"Mean, Median, Mode, and Range." PurpleMath. N.D. https://www.purplemath.com/modules/meanmode.htm. Accessed on November 30, 2019.

"Using Averages." University of Leicester. N.D. https://www2.le.ac.uk/offices/ld/resources/numerical-data/averages. Accessed on November 30, 2019.

Websites

Common Core State Standards Initiative. http://www.corestandards.org/. Accessed on December 7, 2019.

Data.gov. https://www.data.gov/. Accessed on December 7, 2019.

Chapter 8 Activity

"Ask Dr. Math: Mean, Median, Mode, Range." *The Math Forum*. N.D. http://mathforum. org/library/drmath/sets/select/dm_mean_median.html. Accessed on December 9, 2019.

"Averages: Mean, Median, and Mode." SkillsYouNeed.com. N.D. https://www. skillsyouneed.com/num/averages.html. Accessed on December 9, 2019.

Knoch, J. "A Crash Course on Mean, Median, and Mode." Magoosh Statistics Blog. January 1, 2018. https://magoosh.com/statistics/a-crash-course-on-mean-median-and-mode/. Accessed on December 9, 2019.

Smith, J. "How Do People Use Mode, Mean, and Average Every Day?" Sciencing. March 13, 2018. https://sciencing.com/do-mode-mean-average-everyday-8752223.html. Accessed on December 9, 2019.

"Year 8 Interactive Maths: Mean, Median, and Mode." MathsTeacher.com. N.D. https:// www.mathsteacher.com.au/year8/ch17_stat/02_mean/mean.htm. Accessed on December 9, 2019.

9 Framing the Question

Data that can be used for reporting, evaluation, and decision-making are gathered in various ways. The challenge for media consumers is to evaluate the origins of numbers presented in studies, news reports, advertisements, etc. instead of accepting them at face value. Following a brief discussion about data collection in general, this chapter focuses on the importance of survey development. Readers are reminded that, at least initially, use of surveys for data collection may seem like a relatively simple task—ask questions, record answers, tabulate responses, analyze them to draw conclusions, and then report findings. But the reality is that the entire process is more complicated. Even the initial step, writing survey questions to collect the data needed instead of the data desired, is easier said than done. The activity for this chapter focuses on strategies for writing effective survey questions, offering educators and students opportunities to create and test simple surveys. Questions for reflection and a list of suggested resources completes the chapter.

Why Is This Important?

Taking more than a surface look at the origins of numbers used to justify conclusions drawn or decisions made is a critical media literacy skill in today's world because all too often inaccurate data are used, either intentionally or accidentally, as a justification for something. Thanks to the emphasis that has been placed on data-driven decision-making in recent years, educators know that there are many ways data can be gathered such as reviews of records (e.g., medical, governmental, or academic), observations, focus groups, polls, and surveys. They are also familiar with the accuracy of the old adage, "Garbage in, garbage out," which emphasizes the importance of collecting and working with accurate data. But does that work-specific knowledge transfer to data presented in the media? Additionally, members of the general public including students may just not be as familiar with how data are collected.

As a result, when presented with numbers gathered using various processes, most consumers accept the numbers at face value, seldom questioning how they were collected in the first place. There are multiple examples of situations in which numbers presented to the public as fact were actually pulled out of thin air. For instance, many people believe that in order to stay physically fit, they need to walk 10,000 steps every day. In reality, this number is not based on any scientific research. Rather, it came from the name of a pedometer manufactured in Japan in 1965 which, roughly translated, was "10,000 steps meter." In truth, taking as few as 4,400 steps per day can make a difference in mortality rates and the benefits of walking start to level off after 7,500 steps per day (Calechman).

There are multiple opportunities for numbers that are presented as fact to be tainted, all the way from poorly designed data collection instruments to inadequate data collection procedures. Incorrect analysis of the data, drawing improper conclusions about what the data mean, unclear or misleading reports about the significance of findings, and misinforming consumers through use of misleading data visualizations are other ways consumers may be misinformed. This chapter focuses on the importance of appropriate data collection, specifically survey design, and Chapter 10 targets data visualizations and ways they can be distorted to misinform consumers.

Almost everyone has taken a survey at one time or another. Why is this data collection tool used frequently? Surveys are a relatively inexpensive way to gather information about large populations. Well-constructed surveys provide accurate data that can be analyzed and used to make important decisions about all kinds of things. But when poorly conceived, the data gathered from surveys is pretty useless. Before looking a little closer at survey design, let's review a few examples of surveys gone wrong.

Real Life Examples

Have you ever taken a survey that seemed biased? I have. A division of a state-level department in the state where I live regularly surveys people who use its services to get customer satisfaction feedback. This seems like a great way to reach out to users to gather data that could be used to improve services. In reality, the questions are written in such a way that it's nearly impossible to provide accurate feedback on services that are lacking in some way. As a result, the department publishes glowing reports that are inaccurate and many service users say they have stopped completing the surveys because they realize it's a waste of their time. In this case, the data collected are tainted thanks to the questions that are asked and the way they are structured. It's entirely possible that this is unintentional, the result of limited knowledge about survey design, but it's also possible that the surveys are purposefully designed to show positive results.

Many readers will remember a claim made for years by Colgate-Palmolive that 80% of dentists recommended that their patients use Colgate toothpaste. The obvious conclusion for consumers to draw is that only 20% of dentists recommended a toothpaste other than Colgate, but that turned out to be entirely untrue. The data were collected in a telephone survey and the question asked allowed survey participants to name more than one brand of toothpaste. In other

56   *Framing the Question*

words, while it was true that 80% of the professionals surveyed did name Colgate, they also mentioned other brands of toothpaste. In addition, the people conducting the survey failed to mention that it was being paid for by Colgate-Palmolive, leaving the impression that it was an independent survey (Derbyshire). This example shows the importance of knowing what question was asked and who paid for the survey.

How do consumers know if a survey was conducted properly? Reputable researchers will include a description of the survey process in their report. This description includes why a survey was the preferred method for collecting data, how the survey was designed, the questions asked, how the surveys were administered, and more (Kelly et al.). Information with this level of detail won't be reported in articles citing the research, but the name of the survey, the date it was published, and who conducted it should be mentioned along with either a link to the original work or a bibliographic reference for readers to be able to check out. An example of the kind of methodology information provided by reputable researchers is available in *Americans and Privacy: Concerned, Confused and Feeling Lack of Control Over Their Personal Information*, a Pew Research Center document published in November 2019 and listed below in the Resources section of this chapter.

Classroom Practice

Students make observations and gather data starting at a very young age, but designing and testing data collection instruments is a more sophisticated skill. By the time they reach Grade 6, most students are able to think critically about strategies for developing survey questions that will result in the collection of accurate data. The reason for starting with this type of data collection is that most students have had some previous experience with surveys, making this an opportunity to build on existing knowledge instead of having first to provide instruction in how a less familiar data collection strategy works.

While most—if not all—of your students have taken surveys, it is less likely that they have given much thought to how the survey questions they've responded to are written, tested, or organized. Now is the time to start raising student awareness about how the wording and ordering of survey questions may influence survey results. You might begin asking students to think about surveys they have taken. What was the purpose of these surveys? How were they administered (paper, online, interview, etc.)? What was done with the results?

Bring in sample surveys and ask students to compare and contrast the contents. What kinds of questions are asked? How are they similar and how are they different? Are the questions clearly written or difficult to understand? Are students able to draw any conclusions about biases the survey sponsors might have based on how questions are worded? Have students brainstorm a list of the types of questions they are finding in the sample surveys and why they think variety in question format is needed. Once students are better attuned to survey question design, give them an opportunity to complete the activity described in the next section of this chapter to learn tips for writing good survey questions and try their hand at writing survey questions.

Continue to draw students' attention to ways that data are collected. Model asking questions about numbers reported in articles and other reports. Challenge them to conduct their own data collection. Include activities that ask them to create and use their own surveys and then do something with the results. These activities can also be tied to math concepts covered in Chapters 8, 10, and 11, making it possible to broaden the impact of activities. For instance, Chapter 8 focuses on mean, median, and mode. Once data are collected students can use the information to calculate and analyze averages (if appropriate) and then use information provided in Chapter 10 to create a data visualization designed to report findings.

An important piece of these activities is giving students permission to explore not just accurate use of the data, but also its misuse. Students need to have direct experience with intentional creation of misinformation to be able to know what to look for as they consume information.

Activity Plan

Activity: Data Collection—Data are gathered in various ways. One common strategy is use of surveys. On the surface, this may seem simple—ask questions, record answers, tabulate and analyze results to draw conclusions. But the reality is that writing survey questions to collect the data needed instead of the data desired is easier said than done.

What follows is a description of an activity readers may use themselves or with their students. The full activity plan, including a student handout, is available online in the Instructional Activities section at: http://medialiteracytoday. net. Please feel free to download the activity plan and handout files for ongoing use. This activity can be completed in one or two class sessions depending on the length of the instructional period and students' research skills.

Objective: Students work in teams to review tips for writing survey questions and then work in their teams to create six or more questions of their own.

Standards: CCSS.MATH.PRACTICE.MP3, Grades 6–8

Outline—Set the Stage: Give each student has copy of the **Data Collection Handout.** Remind students that data are used to support claims made in studies, reports, articles, and the like. Ask if they have ever wondered if the data being shared are accurate. Mention that since people collect data, it is possible that the information gathering process might reflect the collectors' personal biases.

Help students brainstorm a list of common data sources (e.g., government records, school records, surveys, interviews, observations). Ask how media consumers might check these sources for accuracy and briefly discuss their ideas. Mention that surveys are a common way to gather information from people and that bias can be built into survey questions.

Lead students in a short brainstorming session to create a class list of types of questions that are found in surveys (e.g., True/False, multiple choice, short

58 *Framing the Question*

answer. Add grid and ranked choice to the list and explain, if needed.). Ask student teams to spend a few minutes in their groups to discuss their ideas about the characteristics of good survey questions. In a class discussion, ask teams to share their ideas. Explain that during this activity students will review tips for writing survey questions and each team will develop at least six good questions.

Outline—Activity: Tell students that there are simple tips anyone can use when writing survey questions that help researchers get the information they need as opposed to the information they might think they want. Use the question writing tips provided in the **Data Collection Handout** or provide your own. Have students read and discuss the tips in their teams. Give them an opportunity to ask clarifying questions. Have students review sample questions (those on the handout or questions you provide), comparing them to the tips and deciding how each question could be improved.

Give teams time to develop at least six good survey questions. They may record those questions in the space provided on the handout. Ask them to be prepared to explain why each question is good. Depending on their skill levels and the amount of time required to provide instruction, teams may need a second period to complete the assignment.

Possible Modification: Depending on your students' skill levels and available time, you may decide to walk the class through one or more of the questions before allowing them to work independently.

Have students complete the assignment through the Checking for Understanding section of the handout and then complete the Independent Practice and Reflection sections as homework.

Outline—Extension: Challenge students to use the Extension—Bonus Tips provided on the handout (or create additional tips of your own) to write a short (4–5-question) survey on a topic of personal interest and test the survey by asking 8–10 fellow students to complete it and give feedback on the survey's design.

Questions for Reflection

1. What are the most important ideas presented in this chapter, both for educators and for students?
2. How will you model the skills described in this chapter to ensure your students understand the importance of writing survey questions that result in good data collection?
3. How can you structure learning activities to ensure that students take time to think about how and why data are collected?
4. How will the information presented in this chapter impact your personal efforts to take time to research the origins of numbers reported in media and to determine if those data are accurate?

Resources

Articles

Auxier, B., et al. "Americans and Privacy: Concerned, Confused and Feeling Lack of Control over Their Personal Information." Pew Research Center. November 15, 2019. https://www.pewresearch.org/internet/wp-content/uploads/sites/9/2019/11/Pew-Research-Center_PI_2019.11.15_Privacy_FINAL.pdf. Accessed on January 24, 2020.

Calechman, S. "10,000 Steps a Day—Or Fewer?" *Harvard Health Blog.* July 11, 2019. https://www.health.harvard.edu/blog/10000-steps-a-day-or-fewer-2019071117305. Accessed on January 22, 2020.

Derbyshire, D. "Colgate Gets the Brush Off for 'Misleading' Ads." *The Telegraph.* January 17, 2007. https://www.telegraph.co.uk/news/uknews/1539715/Colgate-gets-the-brush-off-for-misleading-ads.html. Accessed on January 24, 2020.

Kelly, K., et al. "Good Practice in the Conduct and Reporting of Survey Research." *International Journal for Quality in Health Care 15*(3): 261–266, May 2003, https://doi.org/10.1093/intqhc/mzg031. Accessed on January 24, 2020.

Websites

Briggs, S. "Surveys 101: A Simple Guide to Asking Effective Questions." https://zapier.com/learn/forms-surveys/writing-effective-survey/. Accessed on January 25, 2020.

Science Buddies. "Designing a Survey." https://www.sciencebuddies.org/science-fair-projects/references/how-to-design-a-survey. Accessed on January 25, 2020.

SurveyMonkey. "Writing Good Survey Questions." https://www.surveymonkey.com/mp/writing-survey-questions/. Accessed on January 25, 2020.

Chapter 9 Activity

MathisFun.com. "How To Do a Survey." https://www.mathsisfun.com/data/survey-conducting.html. Accessed on January 25, 2020.

Purdue University. "Creating Good Interview and Survey Questions." https://owl.purdue.edu/owl/research_and_citation/conducting_research/conducting_primary_research/interview_and_survey_questions.html. Accessed on January 25, 2020.

TechnoKids. "Survey Questionnaire Ideas for Students Using Google Forms." https://www.technokids.com/blog/apps/survey-questionnaire-ideas-for-students-using-google-forms/. Accessed on January 25, 2020.

10 Putting a Slant on Things

Data visualizations are an effective way to present a lot of data in a compact, easy-to-understand format. Unfortunately, it's also very easy to manipulate graphics to distort what they actually represent. This chapter focuses on use of data visualizations such as graphs to present information to consumers. The activity for this chapter provides tips adults and students can use when scrutinizing pictorial representations of data in order to determine their reliability and then use what they've learned to distort one or more existing graphs. Questions for reflection and a list of suggested resources completes the chapter.

Why Is This Important?

In his article, "Why It's So Hard To Pay Attention, Explained By Science," Daniel J. Levitin wrote that as of 2011, people were consuming five times the amount of information they had in 1986. He also stated that in addition to whatever information they dealt with at work, people were routinely processing an additional 34 GB of data outside work hours every day. The problem that arises when dealing with this volume of information isn't that our brains can't process large amounts of data, it's that our brains cannot efficiently differentiate between what's important and what isn't important. This is why people often feel overwhelmed—even exhausted—when trying to digest large amounts of information. And the amount of data we deal with every day has only increased since 2015.

One way to cope with information overload is to use tools that help consumers grasp the meaning of large amounts of data. Techopedia defines *data visualization* as "the process of displaying data/information in graphical charts, figures and bars." The reason for presenting data in this format is that visual representations of complex information make it easier for viewers to grasp its meaning. Consumers may have noticed increased use of graphs, tables, and infographics in newspapers, magazines, on television, and in other media. The good news is that these data visualizations do help make complex data more comprehensible. The bad news is that these visualizations can easily be tweaked to mislead consumers.

Given that data visualizations can be used to inform or misinform, it is critical that media consumers have skills they can employ to critically review graphs and the like. They need to be familiar with tactics for analyzing these images to determine their accuracy. There are common ways that the presentation of data is distorted to change the meaning whether intentionally or unintentionally. For example, the person creating a data visualization may obscure an issue by including too much data or by cherry-picking the data presented. It's also common to confuse media consumers by using misleading titles, annotations, manipulating the x or y-axis, etc. when designing data visualizations (Hogle). Let's take a closer look.

Real Life Examples

Media outlets are increasing their use of data visualizations when presenting information to consumers. How accurately are these data being presented? We assume that published material has been vetted prior to being made public to ensure that it is accurate and bias-free. Unfortunately, whether it's intentional or not, we cannot take these images at face value because they often do not undergo the scrutiny that many of us grew up expecting.

Journalistic standards were not always high. Merriam-Webster states that the term *fake news* was coined nearly 125 years ago, but that identification of untrustworthy news can be traced back even earlier. When the idea of modern newspapers came to fruition in the early 19th century, false news stories were quite popular. Most people realized that these stories were not true; however, in today's world false news is often more difficult to identify than it was previously.

In today's world, it is becoming increasingly difficult to identify false news, in part because its creators are now using data visualizations to lend credence to misleading stories. In 2014, researchers at Cornell University studied the impact that use of a data visualization can have on whether or not consumers believe a news story. They showed a false news story to two groups of people. One group read a version of the story which included a misleading graph. The second group read a story with text that was identical to the first except that the graph had been removed. Just 68% of the people in the second group believed the story, but 97% of the people in the first group thought it was true. Similar studies show comparable results (Chun). This points out the importance of not only recognizing the impact data visualizations can have on media consumers in general, but also the need to offer students opportunities to explore this phenomenon.

Modern examples of inaccurate data visualizations abound online. Many are political in nature, but certainly not all. Here are a few resources you may want to explore.

- Misleading Graphs: Real Life Examples (https://www.statisticshow to.datasciencecentral.com/misleading-graphs/).
- 5 Ways Writers Use Misleading Graphs To Manipulate You (https://venngage. com/blog/misleading-graphs/)
- Figures and Charts (https://writingcenter.unc.edu/tips-and-tools/figures-and-charts/)

62 *Putting a Slant on Things*

- How to Fix the 15 Most Common Infographic Design Mistakes (https://www.columnfivemedia.com/how-to-fix-the-15-common-infographic-design-mistakes)
- When Will Bad Infographics End? (https://stephanieevergreen.com/bad-infographics/)

Classroom Practice

Repeatedly taking the time to scrutinize data visualizations may seem like overkill, but when it comes to understanding information being presented, it's an essential practice. Students need specific instruction in this skill set along with frequent chances to put these strategies into practice. In addition to reviewing data visualizations during math instruction, opportunities to review graphs, tables, and infographics arise in virtually every content area, making it relatively easy to encourage students to view data visualizations with a critical eye on an ongoing basis.

Here are some basic things students need to be on the lookout for when vetting graphs, tables, and infographics.

Graphs—A common type of data visualization, graphs make it possible to display a lot of information in an easy-to-understand way. This enables consumers to make comparisons and see trends. The meaning of graphs can be misrepresented by:

- Using the wrong type of graph (e.g., pie chart that should be a bar graph).
- Changing the values on the y-axis so they are too big or too small, skipping values, or starting with a number other than zero.
- Missing or incorrect labels.
- Missing or misleading titles.
- Pie chart slices don't add up to 100%.
- Incorrect sizes of slices in pie charts.
- Cherry-picked data.
- Distorting visual perspective using 3-D graphs.
- Inaccurately sizing images used in the graph to distort the numbers they represent.

Tables—Simple tables are a clean way to present data consumers need to understand the information being provided. The meaning of a table may be distorted due to:

- Missing or misleading titles.
- Missing or misleading labels for columns and rows.
- Unidentified data sources.
- Providing too much information.
- Inconsistent formatting of values (e.g., number of decimal places varies).
- Unexplained abbreviations.

Infographics—Well-designed infographics tell a story, but misleading or poorly constructed infographics can distort information. The meaning of an infographic may distorted by:

- Including incorrect or misleading graphs or tables in the infographic.
- Requiring too much scrolling to get through the infographic.
- Visually cluttered and/or disorganized (e.g., too many images, typefaces, colors).
- Lack of structure.
- Missing titles and/or labels.

The activity for this chapter offers a model you can use to help students identify issues not only with graphs, but also in tables and infographics. It's also important to challenge students to manipulate the appearance of accurate graphs, tables, and infographics to help them understand how easily the meaning can be distorted while still using accurate data.

Activity Plan

Activity: Data visualizations—Data visualizations are images that represent data. Graphs, a type of data visualization, are an effective way to present a lot of data in a compact, easy-to-understand format. Unfortunately, it's also very easy to manipulate graphs to distort what they actually represent.

What follows is a description of an activity readers may use themselves or with their students. The full activity plan, including a student handout, is available online in the Instructional Activities section at: http://medialiteracytoday. net. Please feel free to download the activity plan and handout files for ongoing use. This activity can be completed in one or two class sessions depending on the length of the instructional period and students' research skills.

Objective: Students work in teams to use strategies presented by their teacher to enable them to take a close look at graphs in order to determine their reliability. Then students use what they've learned to distort one or more graphs.

Standards: CCSS.MATH.PRACTICE.MP3, Grades 6–8

Outline—Set the Stage: Make sure each student has a copy of the **Data Visualizations Handout**. If students are to draw their graphs by hand, distribute graph paper. If they are to use an online graphing tool, they will need an Internet-connected device.

Remind students that data visualizations are images that represent data and that graphs, which are a type of data visualization, are used to present a lot of data in a compact, easy-to-understand format. Mention that sometimes people who use graphs to illustrate a point may manipulate the graph in ways that mislead viewers. Explain that this manipulation may be intentional or accidental, but it's their job as consumers to think critically about information being presented to them.

Explain that this activity focuses on three types of graphs: bar, pie, and line. Direct students' attention to the Graph Terms section of the handout and ask

64   *Putting a Slant on Things*

them to review the common elements of these types of graphs, giving them a few minutes to read and answer the questions in the Graph Terms section of the handout.

Outline—Activity: Explain to students that there are many ways to distort the meaning of graphs. Share the following list with them:

- Using the wrong type of graph (e.g., pie chart that should be a bar graph).
- Changing the values on the y-axis so they are too big or too small, skipping values, or starting with a number other than zero.
- Missing or incorrect labels.
- Missing or misleading titles.
- Pie chart slices don't add up to 100%.
- Incorrect sizes of slices in pie charts.
- Cherry-picked data.
- Distorting visual perspective using 3-D graphs.
- Inaccurately sizing images used in the graph to distort the numbers they represent.

Use the two graphs found in the Instruction section of the handout or provide similar graphs of your own that students can review and discuss. The discussion can be based on the two questions provided or using your own questions. Two additional pairs of graphs with accompanying questions are provided in the handout. Allow students to review and discuss these or provide graphs and questions of your own. Close the activity by challenging students to gather data using a simple survey they create, design two graphs to represent the results (one accurate and one inaccurate), and present their work to the class.

Possible Modification: Depending on your students' skill levels and available time, you may decide to walk the class through all of the questions together.

Have students complete the assignment through the Guided Practice section and then complete the Independent Practice and Reflection sections as homework.

Outline—Extension: Ask students to find examples of misleading graphs in print or online. Have them explain what's wrong with the graph as presented and what could be done to make the graph represent the data honestly.

Questions for Reflection

1. What are the most important ideas presented in this chapter, both for educators and for students?
2. How will you model the skills described in this chapter to ensure your students recognize the importance of closely reviewing data visualizations to check for accuracy?

3. How can you structure learning activities to ensure that students take time to think about how and why data visualizations can be used to misinform consumers?

4. How will the information presented in this chapter impact your personal efforts to take time to closely review data visualizations to check for accuracy?

Resources

Articles

Chun, R. "The Dangers of Fake News Spread to Data Visualization." Media Shift. February 23, 2017. http://mediashift.org/2017/02/the-dangers-of-fake-news-spread-to-data-visualization/. Accessed on February 4, 2020.

CITS. "A Brief History of Fake News." 2020, https://www.cits.ucsb.edu/fake-news/brief-history. Accessed February 4, 2020.

Evergreen, S. "When Will Bad Infographics End?" Evergreen Data. https://stephanieevergreen.com/bad-infographics/. October 16, 2019. Accessed on February 1, 2020.

French, K. "How to Fix the 15 Most Common Infographic Design Mistakes." Column Five Media. N.D. https://www.columnfivemedia.com/how-to-fix-the-15-common-infographic-design-mistakes. Accessed on February 1, 2020.

Hogle, P. "Misleading Data Visualizations Can Confuse, Deceive Learners." Learning Solutions. August 15, 2018. https://learningsolutionsmag.com/articles/misleading-data-visualizations-can-confuse-deceive-learners#:~:text=of%20clear%20communication.-,Whatever%20the%20reason%2C%20misleading%20data%20visualizations%20have%20no%20place%20in,visualization%20can%20mislead%20learners%20are%3A&text=Hiding%20relevant%20data-,Presenting%20too,Distorting%20the%20presentation%20of%20data. Accessed on January 31, 2020.

Levitin, D.J. "Why It's So Hard To Pay Attention, Explained By Science." *Fast Company*. September 23, 2015. https://www.fastcompany.com/90455663/why-the-ceo-of-ralph-lauren-is-bullish-on-rent-the-runway-and-the-realreal. Accessed on January 30, 2020.

Mansky, J. "The Age-Old Problem of 'Fake News'." *Smithsonian Magazine*. May 7, 2018. https://www.smithsonianmag.com/history/age-old-problem-fake-news-180968945/. Accessed on February 4, 2020.

McCready, R. "5 Ways Writers Use Misleading Graphs to Manipulate You." Venngage. September 11, 2018. https://venngage.com/blog/misleading-graphs/. Accessed on February 1, 2020.

Merriam-Webster, Incorporated. "The Real Story of 'Fake News'." *Merriam Webster*. N.D. https://www.merriam-webster.com/words-at-play/the-real-story-of-fake-news. Accessed on February 4, 2020.

"Misleading Graphs: Real Life Examples." Statistics How To. January 24, 2014. https://www.statisticshowto.datasciencecentral.com/misleading-graphs/. Accessed on February 1, 2020.

Techopedia. "Data Visualizations." 2020, https://www.techopedia.com/definition/30180/data-visualization. Accessed on January 30, 2020.

The Writing Center. "Figures and Charts." University of North Carolina at Chapel Hill. N.D. https://writingcenter.unc.edu/tips-and-tools/figures-and-charts/. Accessed February 1, 2020.

66 *Putting a Slant on Things*

United Nations Economic Commission for Europe. "Making Data Meaningful Part 2: A Guide to Presenting Statistics." 2009. http://www.unece.org/fileadmin/DAM/stats/documents/writing/MDM_Part2_English.pdf. Accessed on February 1, 2020.

Yuan, K. and Peterson, M. "The History of 'Fake News' in America." *The Atlantic.* January 9, 2018. https://www.theatlantic.com/membership/archive/2018/01/the-history-of-fake-news-in-america/550103/. Accessed on February 4, 2020.

Chapter 10 Activity

"Data Visualizations and Misrepresentation." YouTube, 2020. https://www.youtube.com/watch?v=x-rDVXVwW9s. Accessed on February 1, 2020.

Gaslowitz, L. "How to Spot a Misleading Graph." 2020, https://ed.ted.com/lessons/how-to-spot-a-misleading-graph-lea-gaslowitz. Accessed on February 1, 2020.

Interactive. "Bar Graph." 2020, http://www.shodor.org/interactivate/activities/BarGraph/. Accessed on February 1, 2020.

11 What Are the Chances?

Probability, how likely something is to happen, enables us to make reason-based decisions about many aspects of our lives. Whether predicting the results of a roll of the dice, using poll results to determine a proposed law's likelihood to be passed, or looking at a weather forecast to see what clothing to put out for tomorrow morning, we are relying on the probability that something will or will not happen. But predictions are not infallible. This chapter provides an overview of four common types of probability. The activity that accompanies this chapter offers adults and students an opportunity to learn about probability and then apply what they've learned to make predictions. Questions for reflection and a list of suggested resources completes the chapter.

Why Is This Important?

Flip a coin. The chance of it landing tails up is 50%. Flip the coin again. The chance of it landing tails up again is 50%. Flip the coin a third time. The chance of it landing heads up a third time is still 50%. It does not matter how many times a coin is flipped, the chance of it landing tails up remains 50% every time. Why is this so?

It is possible to accurately predict the outcome of tossing a coin multiple times thanks to something called *classical probability*. *APA Dictionary of Psychology* defines classical probability as "an approach to the understanding of probability based on the assumption that any random process has a given set of possible outcomes and that each possible outcome is equally likely to occur." Assuming that the coin has not be altered in some way, there are just two possible outcomes each time the coin is flipped: heads or tails. In other words, the chance of the coin landing tails up is one in two or ½. If you toss a coin 100 times, it will probably land tails up close to 50% of the time. You can easily test this by tossing a coin yourself or by using a coin toss simulator like this one from Shodor at http://www.shodor.org/interactivate/activities/Coin/.

Rolling what is called a "fair" die, meaning that it hasn't been loaded by weighting it in some way, is another example of classical probability. There is an equal probability that when thrown, the die will land on 1, 2, 3, 4, 5, or 6 because a die has six sides numbered 1 through 6. A third example is pulling a particular card from a complete deck. In this instance there is a 1 in 52 chance of drawing one specific

68   *What Are the Chances?*

card (e.g., the Ace of Hearts). This is because there are 52 cards in a complete deck. Given the definition of classical probability, it is easy to make accurate predictions about outcomes based on an easily defined number of possible outcomes.

People tend to like predictability. We want to make decisions based on what we think will happen. Unfortunately, not all outcomes are as certain as those that fall in the category of classical probability. A second type of probability, called *frequentist probability*, defines the likelihood "of some event in terms of the relative frequency with which the event tends to occur" (Pezzullo). The frequentist approach is based on the assumption that it is possible to design an experiment that relies on events that can be replicated many times under the same conditions, to see how often we get the result we want. Scientific studies such as drug trials are designed based on frequentist probability.

A third type of probability is called *subjective probability* and is defined as judgments based on "people's evaluations of the probability of uncertain events or outcomes" (Bar-Hillel). This type of probability is far more common than you might think—weather reports are based on subjective probability as are polls of any kind. Interestingly, while this type of probability is the least scientific of those described above, many people trust subjective probability over more scientific approaches to making predictions. We've all heard about people who have a "system" they use to win at Poker or Blackjack. However, successful gamblers understand that winning requires an in-depth knowledge of probability and statistics. The odds are not in the casual gambler's favor, yet amateurs are often convinced they can use some kind of trick that will enable them to beat the odds and walk away winners (Akusobi).

The fourth type of probability introduced in this chapter is *conditional probability*, which is defined as, "… the likelihood of an event or outcome occurring, based on the occurrence of a previous event or outcome" (Barone). For example, place three yellow paperclips and three red paperclips into a cloth bag and ask someone to pull one paperclip from the bag. Will that person take out a red paperclip when drawing blindly? On the first draw, the chance of them selecting a red paperclip is 3 in 6. Let's say that they do choose a red paperclip—which is put aside—what are the odds of them pulling another red paperclip out of the bag? Now the chances of doing so have changed. Since a red paperclip was drawn the first time, the odds of choosing another one on the second round are 2 in 5 while the odds of selecting a yellow paperclip are now 3 in 5. In other words, the results of the second paperclip draw are dependent on the results of the first paperclip draw. And the results of a third, fourth, and fifth paperclip draw will depend on the results of the previous draws.

Real Life Examples

An impending hurricane sparks mandatory evacuation orders, but some people refuse to leave their homes because they are confident they can ride out the storm safely as they have in the past. Parents refuse to have their children vaccinated because they believe that the odds of the child experiencing serious side effects from vaccinations are much higher than they actually are. Or, a teenager breaks their leg in a fall after taking a dare to climb an unstable structure, having over-estimated their own physical strength and how much time it will take for the structure to collapse. Probability is a critical concept to grasp because we regularly make life altering decisions based on predictions of what we think is going to happen. Here are real-world examples of the four types of probability introduced above.

Example of classical probability—The pros and cons of multiple choice tests have been debated for years, but one of the common objections to these tests is that students can guess their way to a passing grade. Typically, multiple choice questions have four possible answers: A, B, C, or D. Assuming that the test-taker does not use a pattern when selecting answers, each option has a 1 in 4 chance of being selected. This means that, barring penalties for marking incorrect answers, it is possible for someone taking a test to end up with a score that does not reflect their actual level of knowledge about the material covered in the test.

Example of frequentist probability—An education researcher hypothesizes that starting the school day 30 minutes later at high schools would increase attendance rates. The researcher identifies a group of schools to test the hypothesis, and divides them into a test group that changes its schedule to begin 30 minutes later than the current start time and a control group that continues with the existing schedule. At the end of the experiment—say one school year—the researcher compares attendance rates from previous school years to attendance rates for the year being studied to see if attendance increases significantly among the test group schools over that of schools in the control group. This is a simplistic explanation. Other factors might need to be adjusted for, but you get the idea. Bottom line, frequentist probability suggests it is possible to make reasonable predictions based on multiple replicable events.

Example of subjective probability—On Election Day it's not uncommon for people to decide not to vote because pundits using exit polls project winners even before the poll locations close or votes have been counted. Nate Silver, founder and editor in chief of FiveThirtyEight, cites multiple reasons why exit polls are not trustworthy, ranging from the composition of the sampling group to the size of the margin for error in these polls (Silver). In other words, the results of an election may be impacted by decisions made based on limited or even faulty data. Silver actually advises that people ignore exit poll results altogether!

Example of conditional probability—A randomly sampled group of 150 middle school students in Grades 6, 7, and 8 (50 students from each grade level) are surveyed to find out how often they took advantage of a voluntary weekly

70   *What Are the Chances?*

after-school homework help program during the last 10-week grading period. Survey results are shown here:

Table 11.1 Survey Results

Grade Level	0 Times	1–4 Times	5–10 Times	Total
6th	13	12	25	50
7th	20	15	15	50
8th	10	10	30	50
Total	43	37	70	150

Let's say that Grade 8 teachers want to know how likely it is that one of their students attended the after-school program five or more times, based on the survey results. The conditions are that the student is in Grade 8 *and* attended the homework help program at least five times. To find the answer to that question, look at the survey results for Grade 8. Thirty students out of the 50 surveyed met both conditions. Calculate the probability by dividing the number of students who reported attending five or more times by the total number of Grade 8 students surveyed, 30/50. The answer is .6. There is a six in ten chance that a given Grade 8 student attended the program at least five times.

Classroom Practice

Many adults do not understand different types of probability and what they represent, so it's not a surprise that students often struggle with these concepts. And yet adults and students regularly make decisions about important issues based on what they think is likely to happen, often relying on questionable or completely wrong information. Given this reality, what can educators do to help students develop a better understanding of different kinds of probability and why it's important for them to really grasp what probability is about. Here are a few suggestions.

1. Rational decision-making is a critical life skill—People make decisions every day, many of which are predicated on perceived relative risk. Is purchasing a lottery ticket a wise investment? Do the benefits of taking a medication outweigh the risks of side effects that may be caused by that medication? How risky is it for parents to allow their children to ride in the front seat of a car before they reach the age of 13? Help students understand the importance of using reliable predictions when making decisions and how to identify trustworthy sources.
2. Some predictions are more reliable than others—All predictions are not equal. Classical probability may be most reliable when making a prediction, but it is restricted to situations with clearly defined outcomes. Frequentist probability is based on recurring, replicable events that should result in reliable predictions, but it is only as good as the design of the experiment.

Subjective probability is least likely to result in consistently accurate predictions because it is based on opinion which cannot be objectively measured. And conditional probability identifies likely outcomes depending upon certain conditions already being in place. Help students learn to identify the type of probability used to make a prediction when evaluating how reliable that prediction may be.

3.   Every educator has opportunities to help students understand probability in real world contexts—It may be helpful to introduce various kinds of probability using classic examples like flipping coins or drawing marbles from a bag, but students don't see these examples as being relevant to them. Help students understand relevance by extending learning activities to real life situations where probability is used to make predictions.

Activity Plan

Activity: Probability is an idea that enables us to make reason-based decisions about many aspects of our lives. From predicting heads-or-tails when flipping a coin or using poll results to determine a proposed law's likelihood to be passed to looking at a weather forecast to see what clothing to lay out for the morning, we are relying on the probability that something will or will not happen. But predictions are not infallible.

What follows is a description of an activity readers may use themselves or with their students. The full activity plan, including a student handout, is available online in the Instructional Activities section at: http://medialiteracytoday. net. Please feel free to download the activity plan and handout files for ongoing use. This activity can be completed in one or two class sessions depending on the length of the instructional period and students' research skills.

Objective: Students work in teams to learn about different kinds of probability commonly encountered in the real world and then demonstrate what they have learned by creating a quick start guide (a flyer, pamphlet, video, or other format) that others can use to recognize four types of probability.

Standards: CCSS.MATH.PRACTICE.MP3, Grades 6–8

Outline—Set the Stage: Make sure each student has a copy of the **Probability Handout**. If students will create their products offline, make supplies available to them. If they will create their products online, they will need an Internet-connected device.

Explain to students that the term *probability* refers to how likely it is that an event will occur. If they completed the Unbelievable! Activity remind them of the definition of *plausibility*. If they did not do that activity, define plausibility as appearing to be true or reasonable. Then take a few minutes to discuss the difference between probability and plausibility. The important point for students to grasp in this segment of the activity is that something that's *plausible* may or may not be *probable*.

Outline—Activity: Explain to students that while *probability* refers to making predictions about how likely it is that something will happen, there are different types of probabilities. Some predictions can be made with reasonable assurance that they will be accurate, but others are nothing more than educated guesses. Well-informed consumers of media may not have a deep understanding of statistics, but if they understand the basic idea behind different kinds of probabilities they will be able to recognize how reliable the numbers being reported may be. The four types of probability covered in the handout are: classical, frequentist, subjective, and conditional. Provide a definition and example of each type of probability and brainstorm other examples with students.

Once students have grasped the different types of probability covered in this activity, explain that they will work in teams to plan and create a quick start guide meant to help others decide if the predictions they encounter in the media are likely to be accurate. These guides may be in print, video, poster, infographic, or other format approved by the teacher. Once the quick start guides are completed and checked for accuracy, make them available to a genuine audience.

Possible Modification: Depending on your students' skill levels and available time, you may decide to reduce the number of probability types from four to three or to assign teams one or two probability types, ensuring that all four types are covered.

Outline—Extension: Ask students to find examples of probabilities being cited in print or online and then identify the probability type used and explain why it caught their eye.

Questions for Reflection

1. What are the most important ideas presented in this chapter, both for educators and for students?
2. How will you model the skills described in this chapter to ensure your students take time to think about the type of probability being used to make a prediction and how accurate that prediction is likely to be?
3. How can you structure learning activities to ensure that students take time to think about how they use probability to make decisions?
4. How will the information presented in this chapter impact your personal efforts to take time to closely review predictions you encounter to check for accuracy?

Resources

Articles

Akusobi, C. "Should You Bet On It? The Mathematics of Gambling." *Yale Scientific.* February 25, 2010. http://www.yalescientific.org/2010/02/should-you-bet-on-it-the-mathematics-of-gambling/. Accessed on February 12, 2020.

American Psychological Association. "Classical Probability: Definition." *APA Dictionary of Psychology,* 2020. https://dictionary.apa.org/classical-probability. Accessed on February 10, 2020.

Bar-Hillel, M. "Subjective Probability Judgments." Science Direct. 2001. https://www.sciencedirect.com/topics/computer-science/subjective-probability. Accessed on February 11, 2020.

Barone, A. "Conditional Probability." Investopedia. April 30, 2019. https://www.investopedia.com/terms/c/conditional_probability.asp. Accessed February 13, 2020.

"Can You Predict the Future?" Wonderopolis. N.D. https://www.wonderopolis.org/wonder/can-you-predict-the-future. Accessed on February 10, 2020.

Interactive. "Coin Toss." 2020, Shodor. http://www.shodor.org/interactivate/activities/Coin/. Accessed February 10, 2020.

Pezzullo, J. "Two Views of Probability." *Biostatistics for Dummies.* N.D. https://www.dummies.com/education/science/biology/two-views-of-probability/. Accessed on February 11, 2020.

Silver, N. "Ten Reasons Why You Should Ignore Exit Polls." FiveThirtyEight, 2020. https://fivethirtyeight.com/features/ten-reasons-why-you-should-ignore-exit/. Accessed on February 12, 2020.

Chapter 11 Activity

Flipgrid, 2020. https://info.flipgrid.com/. Accessed on February 19, 2020.

Free Online Dice. "Online Dice and Coin Flip." 2020, https://onlinedicefree.com/. Accessed on February 19, 2020.

Google Slides, 2020. http://slides.google.com. Accessed on February 19, 2020.

National Council of Teachers of Mathematics. "Virtual Spinner." 2020, https://www.nctm.org/Classroom-Resources/Illuminations/Interactives/Adjustable-Spinner/. Accessed on February 19, 2020.

Thinglink, 2020. https://www.thinglink.com/. Accessed on February 19, 2020.

12 Going Forward

I wrote this book because many of the educators I've worked with over the last four years reported that the volume of disinformation they needed to deal with was so overwhelming they didn't know where or how to begin. The driving purpose of the book is to provide guidance to educators who want to increase their own abilities to differentiate between fact and fiction in the media as well as guide their students toward becoming well-informed consumers of media in its many formats. For simplicity's sake, I've stuck to two broad areas—Assessing Words and Assessing Numbers—which are suggested in Daniel Levitin's work (Levitin).

Within each of these areas, I've provided five activities per area that are accessible and applicable across content areas. This approach is designed to ensure that educators are able to incorporate these suggestions as instructional strategies rather than becoming even more content to squeeze into an already overcrowded instructional calendar. Yes, students will need direct instruction in how each strategy works, but that can be accomplished using the activities provided in the book and by sharing responsibility for doing this across disciplines. Once students understand a strategy, they can practice that skill in any class. If educators and their students apply just those strategies in their daily consumption of information, they will be better equipped to recognize disinformation.

It is important to keep these skills fresh by practicing them regularly. The activities in Chapters 2 through 11 include suggestions for additional practice but there are also additional resources that offer ready-to-go instructional activities should educators need them for personal use or with students. Several of these are listed a little later in this chapter. Educators can also use current real life examples to develop their own instructional activities using suggestions provided below. But before we turn our attention to other activities, here are five general reminders for educators and students that warrant repetition.

1. Disinformation appears in many contexts, not just politics. Be a critical consumer of all media, not just topics that are obvious venues for misrepresenting truth.
2. Sites like Facebook, Twitter, Instagram, You Tube, etc. are platforms designed for social interactions. They are not reliable sources of information when it comes to medical advice, unbiased news (local, state, national, or international),

weight loss strategies, psychological guidance, or similar concerns and no amount of vetting will change that.

3. Mainstream newspapers, both local and national, are typically reliable sources of vetted, unbiased news.

4. Local televised news is usually more balanced than 24-hour cable stations that rely on sensationalized stories to boost audience numbers. There are exceptions such as local stations that have been purchased by Sinclair Broadcast Group (Edevane).

5. One of the most prevalent sources of disinformation are people who "Like," re-post, or otherwise distribute disinformation because they do not take the time to fact-check anything they decide to share with others. A rule of thumb to use is if you don't have time to fact-check, don't pass along anything you see or hear online.

A number of reputable sources offer free-of-cost lesson plans educators are welcome to use in their classrooms. Here are some readers can begin with.

- Deepfakes: Exploring Media Manipulation (https://www.oercommons.org/authoring/56539-deepfakes-exploring-media-manipulation/view): This lesson plan is designed for Grades 9 and 10, but can be modified for Grades 6–8. It's important for students to develop a general understanding of what deepfake videos are and how they are being used to spread disinformation.
- Digital Citizenship Curriculum (https://www.commonsense.org/education/digital-citizenship/curriculum?topic=news--media-literacy&grades=6,7,8): Common Sense Media, a trusted source of information for teachers, parents, and students, offers three lesson plans for middle school classrooms that are related to recognizing disinformation.
- Disinformation Nation (https://disinformation-nation.org/): This website is created by the Freedom Forum Institute which is a non-profit that focuses on supporting First Amendment rights for all. The activities on this site specifically target strategies for dealing with propaganda.
- PBS News Hour Extra Lesson plan: How to teach your students about fake news (https://www.pbs.org/newshour/extra/lessons-plans/lesson-plan-how-to-teach-your-students-about-fake-news/): This 50-minute activity introduces middle school students to ten questions they can ask to detect fake news.
- Understanding Fake News (https://www.crf-usa.org/images/pdf/UnderstandingFakeNews.pdf): This lesson plan from the Constitutional Rights Foundation was written for high school students, but can be scaffolded for middle school. It includes tips for identifying disinformation and scenarios students can use to practice applying the tips.

Lesson plans written by others are a fine way to get started, but given the amount of disinformation that is time-sensitive, some ready-made lesson plans are out of date shortly after they are published. What strategies can educators use to develop their own activities for classroom use? What resources are available to them? And why is it important for educators to offer students regular opportunities to practice skills they have learned?

Let's begin with why this is important. Thoughtfully designed practice activities make it more likely that students will gain confidence in their ability to apply a skill or strategy and more accomplished in their application of that skill or strategy. *The Marzano Compendium of Instructional Strategies* (Marzano Research, 2016) includes a category called Structured Practice Sessions which goes beyond rote practice of a newly learned skill or strategy. Of the practices recommended, here are four that relate directly to providing time to practice skills and strategies presented in Chapters 2 through 11:

- Teacher modeling—when appropriate, model use of these skills and strategies in front of your students. Make certain they are aware of what you are doing and why.
- Frequent practice—seize opportunities for students to practice one or more of the skills and strategies themselves, e.g., double-checking numbers in something they read or fact-checking the origin of a quotation.
- Varied practice—create opportunities for students to apply the skills and strategies in challenging situations, e.g., occasionally present a scenario students need to work through, using one or more of the skills/strategies they have learned in a new or different context.
- Ongoing practice—support students' fluent use of a skill or strategy by requiring documentation of their use of one or more of these skills in independent assignments they complete.

Based on the general kinds of structured practice strategies listed above, it should be clear that this is something educators can do fairly easily. For example, modeling strategies that can help someone recognize disinformation does not necessarily require a lot of advance planning. What it does require is starting to think in those terms and taking an extra few minutes to model scrutinizing words and numbers encountered in work students would be doing anyway using the strategies covered in the activities provided in Chapters 2 through 11.

Frequent and varied practice can also be included in activities your students already complete such as current events, short daily reviews at the start or close of class, textbook chapter walks, etc. As is the case with modeling, these review activities are often more a case of remembering to emphasize these information literacy skills than having to spend a lot of time creating new activities.

Implementation of ongoing practice may require educators to review independent activities to ensure they provide opportunities to practice these information literacy skills and modify those that do not. It may also be necessary to create a rubric students can use when documenting their use of these skills during the independent activity. If so, there are a number of free online rubric generators that make designing a rubric quick and easy. For example, iRubric (https://www.rcampus.com/indexrubric.cfm) or RubiStar (http://rubistar.4teachers.org/index.php).

Going Forward 77

There is no shortage of disinformation educators can use as the basis for classroom activities, but it can be helpful to have ideas delivered directly to your email box. My favorite idea resource is The Sift Newsletter from the News Literacy Project (https://newslit.org/educators/sift/). Published weekly throughout the traditional school year, this free weekly newsletter includes: articles to share with students along with discussion questions; viral rumor rundowns featuring images and annotated text that explains why a viral rumor is true or false; and multiple ideas for classroom lessons. Educators who like the idea of creating their own lessons—which can be used for ongoing practice—but who would like a ready-to-use format are welcome to use or adapt the Lesson Plan Template (https://www.sjbrooks-young.org/wp-content/uploads/2020/03/Lesson-Plan-Template.docx) that was used to create the activity plans included in the online resources for this book. For another point of view regarding how to develop a classroom project focused on fake news, take a look at classroom teacher Gil Teach's short article describing how she approached writing a week-long unit to help her students learn to recognize disinformation. It is available at http://gilteach.com/2017/01/12/designed-fake-news-lessons-plans/.

This is a challenging, yet exhilarating time to be an educator. So much is happening in the world and everything we thought we knew about information literacy has proven to be in constant flux. I hope you will use the material in this book as a springboard for navigating your way through the constantly changing information landscape that faces us and our students. Remember that this challenge can be addressed by applying critical thinking skills, understanding civics, and developing information literacy skills. We can do this.

Resources

Articles

Burston, A. et al. "A Citizen's Guide to Fake News." Center for Information Technology & Society, University of California Santa Barbara. August 29, 2018. https://www.cits.ucsb.edu/fake-news. Accessed on March 8, 2020.

"Digital Citizenship Curriculum: Grades 6–8." Common Sense Media, 2020. https://www.commonsense.org/education/digital-citizenship/curriculum?topic=news--media-literacy&grades=6,7,8. Accessed on March 8, 2020.

"Disinformation Nation." Freedom Forum Institute, 2020. https://disinformation-nation.org/. Accessed on March 8, 2020.

Edevane, G. "Is Your Local News Station Owned By Sinclair? What You Need To Know about Efforts To #BoycottSinclair." *Newsweek.* April 2, 2018. https://www.newsweek.com/my-station-owned-sinclair-boycott-868305. Accessed on March 5, 2020.

Ferguson, S. "Deepfakes: Exploring Media Manipulation." OER Commons. August 6, 2019. https://www.oercommons.org/authoring/56539-deepfakes-exploring-media-manipulation. Accessed on March 8, 2020.

"Get Smart About News." News Literacy Project, 2020. https://newslit.org/get-smart/. Accessed on March 7, 2020.

78   *Going Forward*

"Lesson Plan: How to Teach Your Students about Fake News." PBS News Hour Extra, 2020. https://www.pbs.org/newshour/extra/lessons-plans/lesson-plan-how-to-teach-your-students-about-fake-news/. Accessed on March 8, 2020.

"Lesson Plan Template." Media Literacy Today, 2020. https://www.sjbrooks-young.org/wp-content/uploads/2020/03/Lesson-Plan-Template.docx. Accessed on March 8, 2020.

"Structured Practice Sessions." The Marzano Compendium of Instructional Strategies, 2020. https://www.marzanoresources.com/online-compendium-product/. Accessed on March 8, 2020.

Teach, G. "How I Designed My Fake News Lessons Plans." 2017. http://gilteach.com/2017/01/12/designed-fake-news-lessons-plans/. Accessed on March 8, 2020.

"The Sift." News Literacy Project, 2020. https://newslit.org/educators/sift/. Accessed on March 7, 2020.

"Understanding 'Fake News'." Constitutional Rights Foundation. 2017. https://www.crf-usa.org/images/pdf/UnderstandingFakeNews.pdf. Accessed on March 8, 2020.

Books

Levitin, D.J. *Weaponized Lies: How to Think Critically in the Post-Truth Era.* New York: Dutton, 2017.

Websites

iRubric. Reazon Systems, Inc.., 2020 https://www.rcampus.com/indexrubric.cfm? Accessed on March 8, 2020.

RubiStar. 4Teachers.org, 2020. http://rubistar.4teachers.org/index.php. Accessed on March 8, 2020.

Index

Adams, J. 27
advertisements 2
Advertising Standards Authority (ASA) 1
Akusobi, C. 68
algorithms 21
Allen, Ben 20
"alternate facts" 1
Anderson, J. 3
anti-Vax groups 1
autism 8
averages 47–52

Bar-Hillel, M. 68
Barnum, P. T. 7
Barone, A. 68
Bartles, L. 34
Bergson-Michelson, T. 9
bias 55
bin Laden, Osama 7–8
bonafide experts 15
Borel, B. 34
Boston Marathon bombing 41
bots 35
browsers 22, 36
Burston, A. et al. 1

cable-news networks 14, 75
caches 22
Can't Confirm That Quotation? 9
Capatides, C. 1
card games 67–68
causation 42
CBC Kids News 28
Charlton, Graham 21
"Cherry Tree Myth" 7
childhood vaccines 8
Chun, R. 61
citizenship 3
citizenship journalism 40–41

civics 2, 3
Clarke, S. 27
classical probability 67, 69, 70
clickbait 2
CNN 14
coin toss simulators 67
Common Sense Media 3, 75
conditional probability 68, 69–70, 71
confirmation bias 19, 20
conspiracy theories 27, 29–30
consumers 33
contextomy 8
cookies 22
correlations 42
Coulter, P. 15
counterknowledge 26–31, 33, 36–37
COVID-19 1
credibility 12, 15

data collection 54–55; survey design
    54–58
data visualization 40, 41, 55, 60–64, 71;
    see also statistics
D'Costa, K. 27
decision-making 70
deepfakes 28, 38, 75
DeGroat, T. J. 50
Derbyshire, D. 56
dice 67
dictionaries 12, 13, 16, 42, 67
Digital Citizenship Curriculum 75
disinformation 2, 26, 27, 28, 29, 33, 35,
    74, 76, 77
Disinformation Nation 75
Dreyfuss, E. 2
drug trials 68

echo chambers 19, 21–23
Edevane, G. 75

80　*Index*

election results 69
empathy 22
Ereku, M. H. 12, 13
estimation 43
Evon, D. 33
exit polls 69
experiment 68–70
expert opinion 12, 14–17

Facebook 1
Fact Checker 34
fact-checking 15, 27–28, 34–36, 38, 76
fake news 1–2, 33, 61, 75, 77
fake photos 35
fake posts 34
false consensus effect 19, 20
First Amendment rights 75
Fisher, M. 1
Fox 14
Freedom Forum Institute 75
frequentist probability 68, 69

gambling 68
Gobet, F. 12, 13
Google 22
Google Books 9
Google reverse image search 36
graphs 41, 51, 60–64
Gross, D. 34

hackers 28
Halsey, N. 8
headlines 2
Hogan, J. 42
Hogle, P. 61
How to Research a Quotation 9
Hurricane Sandy 40–41

"illusory truth effect" 2
image searches 36
inaccurate information 26–31
infographics 63
information echo chambers 19–24, 28
information literacy skills 2–4, 76–77
Interactive Media Bias Chart 29
Internet news sources 21
Internet searches 22
Internet trolls 35

Jaffe, E. 2
JFK assassination conspiracy theory 30
journalistic standards 61

Kelly, K. 56
King, Martin Luther 7–8
Kirtley, J.E. 1
Konnikova, M. 26

lesson plans 75–76
Levitin, D.J. 4, 7, 60, 74
Lieb, G. 7
local news stations 75
"lying press" 1

Madrigal, A. C. 34
Marble, Vicki 35
marijuana sales 34–35
Marzano Compendium of Instructional Strategies 76
Matthews, J. 2
McNamara, Robert 26–27
mean average 47, 49
media consumers 33
media literacy 54
median 47–51
MediaSmarts 28
mental math 43
misinformation 8–9, 26–29, 33, 36–37, 41, 51, 57
misleading claims 41–42
misleading correlations and causation 42
misleading data visualizations 41, 55, 64
misquotation 7
Mitchell, A. 14, 21, 27
mode 48–51
MSNBC 14
multiple choice tests 69
myths 7

National Report 34
Nazi Germany 1
newscasts 14
NewsFeed Defenders 35
News Literacy Project 35
newspapers 21, 23, 61, 75
news sources 21, 23, 28, 75
number sense 42–44

online news sources 21
online shopping 21
O'Toole, G. 7, 10

Parkinson, R. G. 27
permission to forget 50
personal information bubbles 19–21

Pew Research Center 14, 21, 27, 56
Pezzullo, J. 68
pie charts 41
plausibility 40–45, 71
playing cards 67–68
poll results 69, 71
poverty 19
predictions 68–72
probability 67–72
problem-solving strategies 43
pseudoscience/pseudohistory 31
pundits 13–15, 69

quotations 6–10
Quote Investigator 9

radio 2, 14, 21, 23
Rainie, L. 3
rational decision-making 70
Red Bull 2
Resnick, A. 28
responsible citizenship 3
reverse image search 36
Robb, A. 28
rubric generators 76

safety net social services 19
search engines 22
Shao, G. 28
Shodor 67
Sift Newsletter 77
Silver, Nate 69
Sinclair Broadcast Group 75
Snopes 34

social media platforms 7, 21, 23, 33, 36–37, 40–41, 74–75
social services 19
spoof articles 34
statistics: misleading claims 41–42; misleading correlations and causation 42; misleading data visualizations 41, 41, 55; plausibility 40–45; probability 67–72
subjective probability 68–69, 71
survey design 54–58

tables 62
Taub, A. 1
Teach, Gil 77
television 2, 4, 21, 23, 27, 41, 60, 75
thinking out loud 43
Thompson, Damien 27, 29
Tripathi, Shashank 34
trolls 35
Trump Administration 1
Twitter 8, 40–41

ultracrepidarians 13
urban myths 35

vaccinations 8, 69
vetting 28
Vigen, Tyler 42
viral posts 7, 34–35, 77

Washington, George 7
Weems, Mason Locke 7
Weir, K. 33
WWJ radio station 14

Printed in Great Britain
by Amazon